DIRTY BLONDE

THE DIARIES OF

COURTNEY LOVE

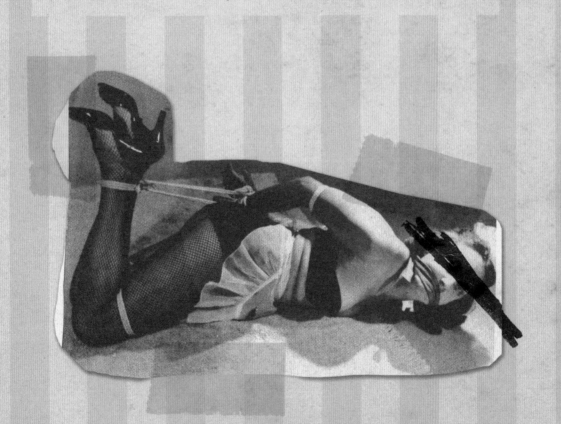

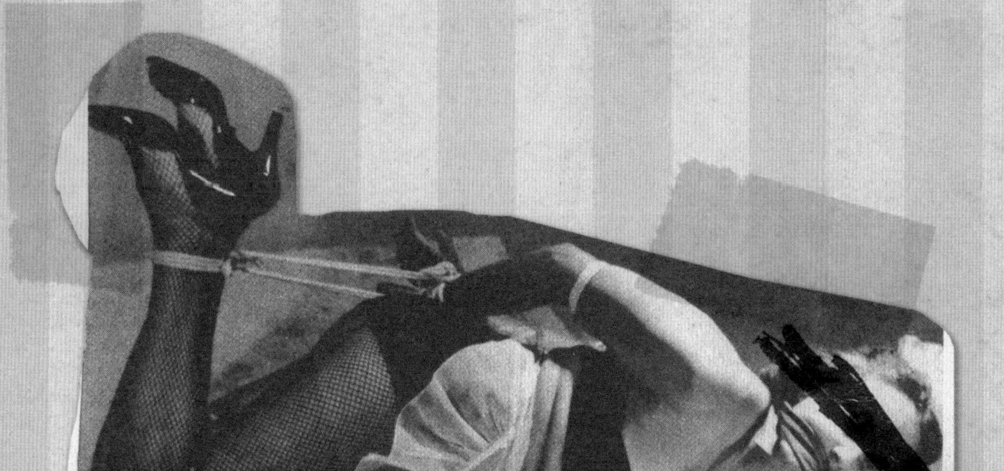

DIRTY BLONDE

THE DIARIES OF

Courtney Love

RESEARCHED AND EDITED BY

AVA STANDER

PICADOR

First published 2006 by Faber and Faber, Inc.
an affiliate of Farrar, Straus and Giroux, New York

First published in Great Britain 2006 by Picador
an imprint of Pan Macmillan Ltd
Pan Macmillan, 20 New Wharf Road, London N1 9RR
Basingstoke and Oxford
Associated companies throughout the world
www.panmacmillan.com

ISBN-13: 978-0-330-44546-7
ISBN-10: 0-330-44546-4

1 3 5 7 9 8 6 4 2

A CIP catalogue record for this book is available from the British Library.

Designed by Paul Kepple, Jessica Hische, Jude Buffum, and Frances Soo Ping Chow @ Headcase Design
www.headcasedesign.com

Printed and bound in Great Britain by
Butler & Tanner Ltd, Frome

CONTENTS

ACKNOWLEDGMENTS

WHEN I DRIFTED OFF TO SEA AND WENT TO THE DARKEST CAVES OF HELL, THESE PEOPLE PULLED ME THROUGH AND UP AND OUT. WITHOUT THEM MY LIFE WOULD SUCK AND I'D BE DEAD:

Frances Bean, Jason Weinberg, Howard Weitzman, Cameron Crowe, Brett Ratner, Deb, Warren Boyd, Mel Gibson, Billy Corgan, Linda Perry, Trudie and Sting, Stacey Sher and Kerry, Edward Norton, Heather Parry, Allison Shearmur, Lisa Leveridge, Neil Strauss, Marie Walsh, Peter Asher, Alan Nierob, Stephen J., Alan McGee, Lisa Moorish, my bandmates Paul, Desmond, and Nate, Kimberly Stewart, Tracey Ross, Milos Forman, Julie Panebianco, Michael Stipe, Bono, Bennett M (who is wondrous in every way), Rand Rubin for not sending me to the pokey, Craig Marks, André Balazs, Phil and everyone at the Chat, Woody Harrelson and Laura Louie, Jolie, the Great Carrie Fisher (mentor & muse), the divine David LaChapelle (and his will to live & create), Marc Jacobs for never ever being reactive and always having a girl's back even when she's down, Lara Shriftman, Heidi & Jill, Mensch for letting me clear the air, Matt Lucas, Sara Sugarman, Agent X at the FBI (for being my knight in shining armor), Guy O, Amanda Demme, Chris Rock, Brandi Rolfe, Vigliano, Steves, sweet Billy Bob for changing my paradigm at the Sunset Marquis, Klaus, Miss Pamela (for being a good friend), Larry Mestel, John Branca, David Byrnes, Frank Rodriguez, Eric Evlandson, my editors Denise Oswald and Ava Stander, Drew & Nan for just being family.

AUTHOR'S NOTE

I HAVE ALWAYS SAID that I would never write a book and I really haven't. This is a collection of what got left behind from my life so far and of what I am willing to share. So many of my things have disappeared in fires (both real and metaphorical) or with movers that some of the choices were already made for me.

I have been asked why I am doing it; I guess it is because after all the black years (and I've had a few) I wanted to define myself for better or worse, how I think and am and behave. My values have changed drastically over the years; I am now a practicing Buddhist, sober and macrobiotic. I have been Catholic, dabbled in Scientology for a moment, and checked out Wiccan books from the Eugene, Oregon, library to cast spells on innocent fourth graders. I've been a shoplifter and an activist and I've been an asshole. What I really want out of this is for the reader to know how I experienced life and thus how I created songs.

I am not reticent when it comes to speaking my mind. I like the fluffy, gracious-living movie star things as anyone would but I am also a real feminist and have a strong political side. You will notice the absence of anything much for about four years of my life; that's because I was on drugs and nothing I wrote made any sense. It may be that for some people their drug years purchased them greatness but mine brought me nothing but dull, aching pain, misery, and wrecked lives—mostly my daughter's. I never grieved properly for the death of my husband and it finally caught up with me in 2000.

I do not kiss and tell, but the wild pirate life I have led gave me many great adventures. I have had a fabulous ride so far—filled with music, hope and glory, tragedy, boys, and lots and lots of poetry.

The greatest gift I was given as a child was being raised without fear. One has to take risks, one has to love oneself and have the courage to ride that ghost into uncharted territory; and in this quest I have been fueled by the blistering desire to make it somehow. At my age, I treasure my past and look forward to the second half of my life. Above all, I thank God for my own child—she is my sun and moon. I am grateful to my friends who rescued me from myself time and time again.

Thanks for giving me the chance to share these scraps and bits and bobs; I have always believed in keeping the pen and the piece of wood with the six strings nearby and writing it all down in a diary or in a song—the shock, the agony, the ugliness, and the beauty, every fucking second of it. There is only one ride and it is a wonderful one.

My last words are simple and written with a straight face: Love really is the answer—love for humanity, love for self, love for family, love for one another, and love for your friends. Love is the highest human function and I am proud to have so many loved ones and to be loved. It makes life worth living.

Blessings,

COURTNEY LOVE

INTRODUCTION

BY

CARRIE FISHER

THERE'S A SAYING: "Some of us can't find heaven without backing away from hell." Well, it seems to me that that's been part of Courtney Love's experience—not that she's found heaven, but I'm sure she has seen glimpses of the place. How could she not, with all her experience fighting her demons? She's had to have had some sweet feelings; possibly even ones she felt were brought to her by angels, who knows? The relief of surviving one's particular hell is often heavenly.

After Kurt died, Courtney did her grieving in public . . . if she did any grieving at all. I've heard that grief is a private thing, but privacy is a far-off Shangri la–like kingdom that Courtney long ago lost her map to. Most would say willingly—and they'd more than likely be right. She did seem to want to capture the attention of the rock and roll world and keep it right in her grasp for all time. And that's the trade-off—privacy for publicity—or so I've heard.

But isn't that the dream of so many people, that dream of stardom? Audiences at your feet, screaming your name, worldwide acclaim, and you up there, above reproach, past caring, the sins of your past wiped clean . . . a miracle! The pain and losses of your childhood not even a memory. *If they could see me now! Wouldn't they be sorry they didn't treat me better! They'll wish they'd never . . . they'll wish they had . . . fame will be a new mother to me; a mother with many heads; one who follows me everywhere, who's interested in everything I do. A mother who clothes me and feeds me and gives me the biggest roof over my head imaginable and an allowance that never quits.*

And for someone who felt unwanted, or unloved, or sent away from home at an early age, and who had been traveling an awfully long time, Mother Fame would look like a homecoming. But I think you want to perform your art in public. At least I imagine Courtney did. Sing her songs or act in her films, not live her life out on a world stage. But that's fame in the twenty-first century. Mother is very strict about that these days. Fame is an around-the-clock affair. You punch in and you never punch out, especially if your life is so interesting that sometimes you can barely fucking breathe. There is said to be a Chinese curse: "May you live in interesting times." Those ancient Asians must have had Courtney, and a few more of us, in mind when they etched out that hex in those faraway times. Because since Kurt's suicide, I can't really remember too long of a time when the press would avert its awful gaze from Courtney. Grieving Courtney, Widow Cobain, Single Mother Courtney, mom to fatherless Frances Bean. Courtney's brilliant new album: Did she write it or did her now-deceased husband? Stoned Courtney: Is she or isn't she? Grieving Courtney: When did that happen? When did she take the time? Courtney as fashion icon: from rocker rags to haute couture. Did she do something to her face or didn't she? Who is Courtney hanging out with? What celebrities? What rock icon is she warring with and why? Billy Corgan or Marilyn Manson? Courtney's filming a movie directed by Milos Forman with Edward Norton and Woody Harrelson: The word is she's very good. Is that true? How can that be? I hear she's dating Edward Norton. No! That can't be true. Where did you hear that? How old is her daughter now? I hear she looks like her dad. I hear Courtney's really badly behaved on the film. Really? I heard the opposite. Who did you talk to? I hear she had to insure herself, that no one would insure her. I hear she carries Kurt's ashes around with her in a teddy bear. No, that's so weird! Are you allowed to do that? I heard she found the body. I heard her father said some awful things about her, like she controlled Kurt or something. Her father? You mean the guy who dropped all that acid and never met Kurt in his life? You know what I think? I think because Kurt looked like this fragile angel and Courtney looks like this tough street chick, people say crazy shit like that. I saw the movie—she's brilliant in it. Awesome! But, I mean, she plays a junkie, so how much of a stretch can that be for her, right? Well, wait, a lot of people are a lot of things, but that doesn't mean they can play them. I hear she bought Ellen Degeneres's house in Coldwater Canyon. Really? Expensive house? Oh yeah, millions, I'm told. Well, I hear her grandmother is a really famous well-respected author who gave up Courtney's mother for adoption, and that her mother is this psychologist who treated some famous radical on the run from the law. Wow. I heard the mom was a nudist and used to go skinny-dipping when Courtney was a kid. I heard rumors and denials that her grandfather is Marlon Brando. I hear she's part Jewish. Wow, did you see that she didn't get nominated? That's kind of weird. Everyone thought she would. Yeah, but I hear she's going to be a presenter on the Oscars this year. That I have to see . . .

And that's when I met Courtney. I was a staff writer for the Academy Awards, she was presenting, and I was assigned to write something that met with her approval, because everyone over at Casa del Oscar imagined Courtney would be a nightmare to deal with. So, I was sent as the diplomat from the Country of Show Business to establish relations with the land of all things Love and Courtney. But contrary to everyone's expectations (I don't know what mine were; I mean, my mother is Debbie Reynolds—how much bigger than that could she be?) I found Courtney to be . . . well . . . I got along great with her. You might say we got along like a house on fire, which would make sense, as you would have to go a fair distance to find two bigger smokers, or two greater masters at burning it down to the ground, than Miss Love and myself. There was a comedy trailer, where the jokes were housed and fed at the back of the Shrine Auditorium, and Courtney immediately moved in. There were changes of clothes, Kurt's mother and sister, love notes from Edward, and more. Everyone watched the telecast on the little TV in the camper and screamed and yelled and jumped on the sofa when Cuba Gooding, Jr., gave his great, long, ecstatic acceptance speech, and later more winnings and losses that, at this distance and having burned too many brain cells, I can no longer remember.

But Courtney's joy is what I first noticed about her. This joyfulness had to be part of this whole crazy star-choked Oscar fest, and how happy she was to be wearing the haute couture and the borrowed jewels, what a goof it was to have arrived at the erstwhile Mecca of Movie Industry. Here at the Oscars. Here in this trailer. Sure, this was a girl of appetites, but she was not a person who always feeds on a gloomy feast.

We discovered that our daughters were the same age, born the same year, divided by a month and a day, and that we lived right next door to each other. Our properties literally shared a border in our backyards. So this was the beginning of my friendship with Courtney. My daughter, Billie, and her daughter, Frances, ultimately became friends. We traveled together to Thailand and to the Orange County Fair—a world of extremes.

That's what I think you'll find in these pages of Courtney's journals. A girl making her way through her life—a far from easy one, to be sure, but she is someone who barely had time for a childhood, who was thrust into this world without appropriate role models or any coping skills. Not unlike many young people of her generation, and generations before, and after, which is one of the reasons why I think her music has enjoyed the popularity it has, as well as being a contributing factor to its amazing critical success.

In these journals you'll find the young Courtney before she surfaced into our choked fishbowl for all the world to see, to sing along with, and to comment on: Courtney under construction, Courtney self-destructing; taking things too hard—to heart, and on the chin. Courtney trying to make sense of things, succeeding, failing. Courtney, the wild child, wise beyond anyone's years, a precocious kid. Courtney with her rampant empathy—a person without insulation. If someone gets a headache in Iquitos, Peru, she feels it in the back of her brain. She picks up radio stations in her molars on a clear night. This is a lady made for those drugs that quiet the noise, that soften that edge. She's the doctor and the patient, and frequently the doctor just isn't in. Over the years, anyone who cares to has been able to watch her struggle with her more-than-medical self-ministrations. With Kurt, and then alone.

But she's always used her writing and her music to make sense of it; first in these journal entries and early wise child lyrics from the age of fourteen, then with music: her band Hole, from their amazing landmark album *Pretty on the Inside*, to their critically acclaimed *Live Through This*, written before the death of her husband, directly after she toured, and then Hole's *Celebrity Skin*, along with Courtney's solo album, *America's Sweetheart*, and finally the newest (and perhaps most remarkable) album, *How Dirty Girls Get Clean*.

This lady, this friend and former neighbor of mine, has healed herself on and off in four ways (that I know of) over the years: with genius men, bad medicine, great music, and motherhood. A rock icon for all seasons.

So these journals are a glimpse into the unhip, unobserved (until now) Courtney Love. After all is said and done—whenever that is—she is a survivor. Unfortunately, the only thing wrong with being a survivor is you have to keep getting in trouble to show off your gift. Getting in trouble and then getting out again, bearing gifts.

—JULY 11, 2006

THE DIARIES

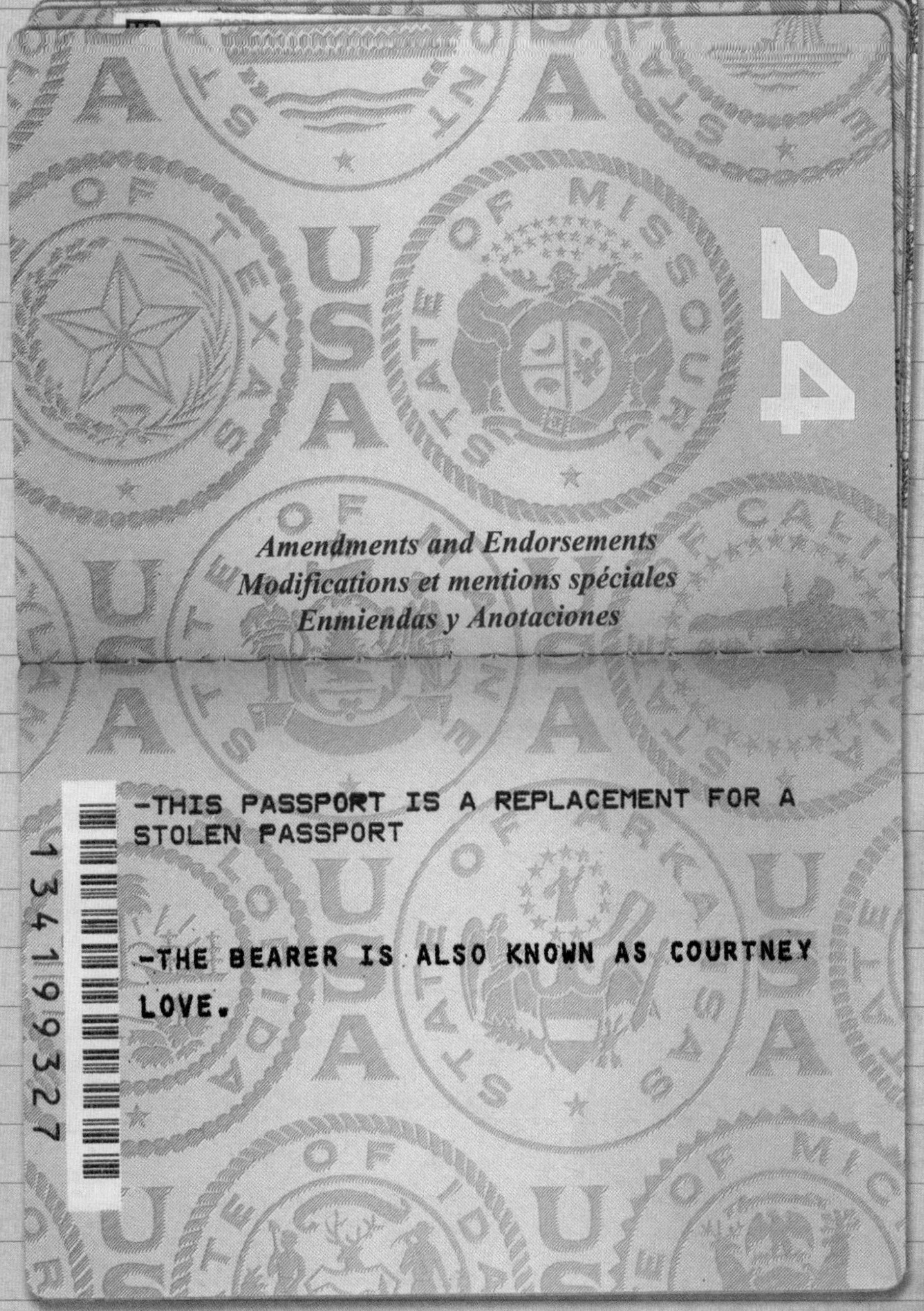
24
Amendments and Endorsements
Modifications et mentions spéciales
Enmiendas y Anotaciones
-THIS PASSPORT IS A REPLACEMENT FOR A STOLEN PASSPORT
-THE BEARER IS ALSO KNOWN AS COURTNEY LOVE.
134119327

Jan28.75 Tuesday
Michelle

me & miss monika
she was a Dutch playboy model.
I was teachers pet

Marcola Oregon, 72, we had just come into a few million dollars. we had to fast on brewers yeast.

Sep 75
C. MR

inflight with
air new zealand

I saw Sally
Struthers (ARCHIE BUNKERS
DAUGHTER) at the L.A. airport.
I saw "The Blackbirds" last night
and "Mr. Quip" tonite.
Everythings fine so far
except one thing.
I will Never go to Tahiti again,
Never Never, that Airport
is Just CRAWLING with
COCKROACHES it was disgusting
hundreds of em' piling up
on each other. I
got a lei. of hibiscus flowers
its in the fridge on the
airport.

inflight with
air new zealand

I'm on a DC-10 looking at
the sunrise out my window
its beautiful! One side
is a beautiful starry night
with a palefaced moon shining
above
and the other side is
Just Beautiful it starts
Ruby Lemon Ruby Red
going into a
indian orange, then pale
lemon yellow, then
Rolling hills green then
a warm, thin Grayish color,
then a watery blue, then
a Richer blue, then sky
Blue then midnight
Blue,

Love

Cartney
Menely c/o
NCG, Hostel
Examiner st.
Nelson New Zealand

July 28th

Guess what! in our school play we are doing Oliver Twist and I'm (Da Da Da, La, La) Fagin! ← I also played the Artful dodger of course.

theres 600 ~~people~~ girls in our school.

Im trying to organize myself I start with my part of the dormitory cleaning, knowing where things are, then on to school, then my mind and let me tell you thats Hard!

Theres a neat T.V. show on called "Ready to Roll" it has all the popstars singing their ~~his~~ songs. its just bits from concerts. etc.
have you got the song "Fernando" by Abba over their yet? I'm so bored with these songs "Shannon" and "Boogie fever" are the top 2!
how Bloody dum-dum-dum.

July 28 on Saturday wed go see "Carry on" movies in town & Sunday was always reserved for Monty python my favorites. ⟶ ~~my~~ my

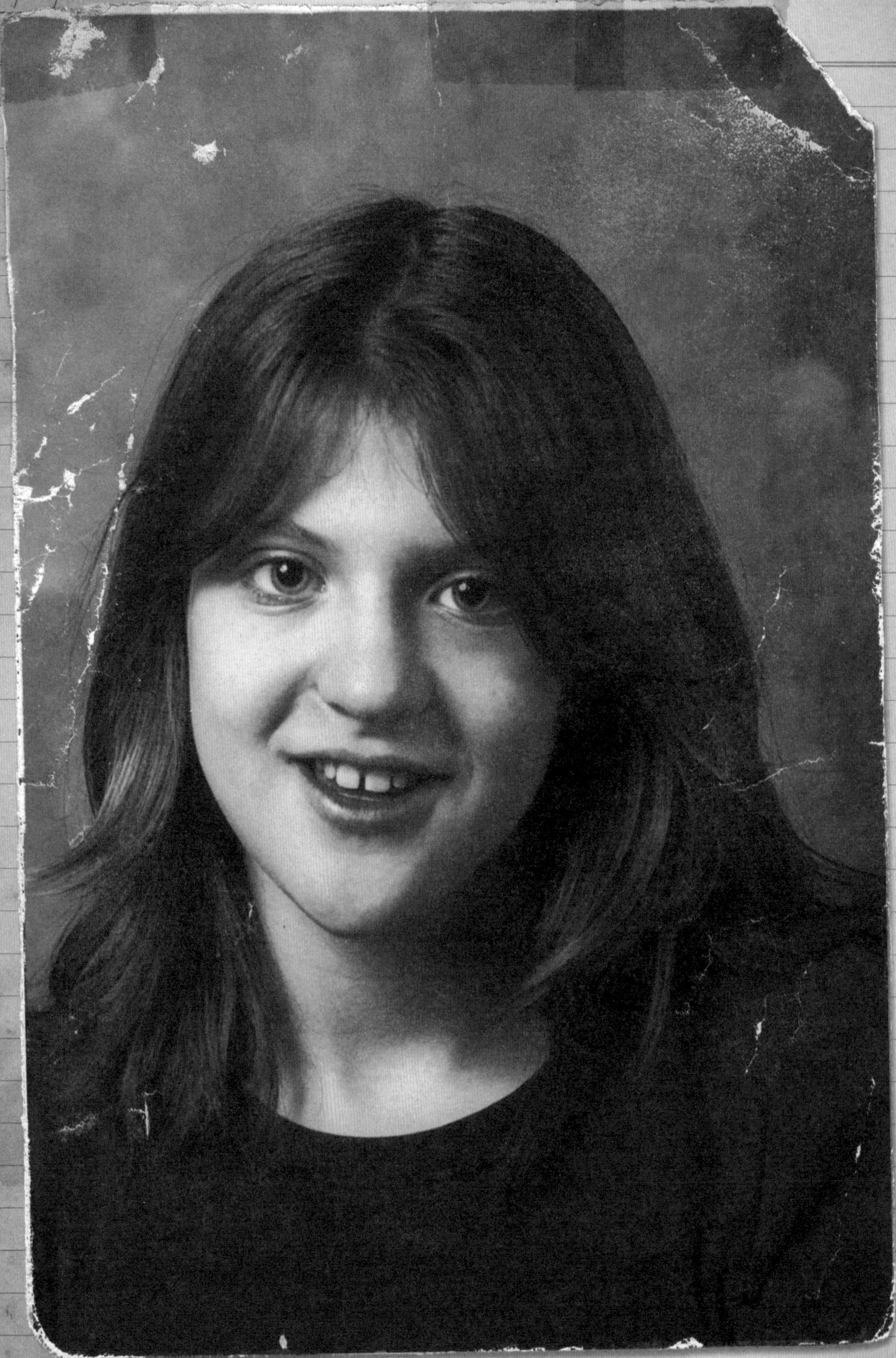

Nellie my 1st dog

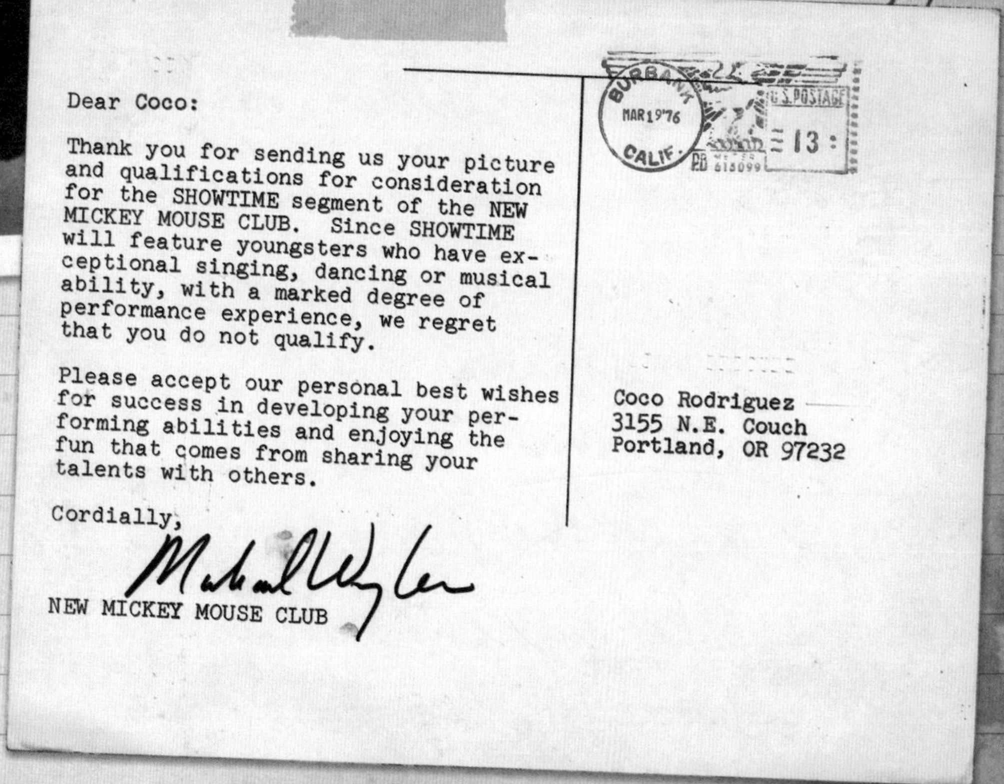

BURBANK CALIF. MAR 19 '76 U.S. POSTAGE 13

Dear Coco:

Thank you for sending us your picture and qualifications for consideration for the SHOWTIME segment of the NEW MICKEY MOUSE CLUB. Since SHOWTIME will feature youngsters who have exceptional singing, dancing or musical ability, with a marked degree of performance experience, we regret that you do not qualify.

Please accept our personal best wishes for success in developing your performing abilities and enjoying the fun that comes from sharing your talents with others.

Cordially,

NEW MICKEY MOUSE CLUB

Coco Rodriguez
3155 N.E. Couch
Portland, OR 97232

* its me,
you know, mouthy,
a little wierd, late on Poberty...

...and my mothers gone nuts
and sent me to Camp Kiwi –
an Evangilacal Born again
Camp wich takes up an entire
Island, a little Island In the
middle of the big Island's of NZ,

the Man is preachin',
he's preaching all sorts
of fire & brimstone –
and all of the sudden my line
across the chairs, scarfs
aloft, tartan on jeans
start screaming
'we want the Rollers –
we want the Rollers'
maybe 20 of us – and yes I am one
of the loudest.
How does a savory ~~smart~~ American Girl find herself
stranded on an Island in NZ screaming
'I want the Rollers' in 19~~77~~?
I've never figured it out –

a year later Im in the American N.West,
Brutal Junior High, No Sweet. No slade. No Bowie,
No Jackie, NO monty python, NO Abba and certainly
No Rollers just alot of Zeppelin Belt Buckles
and interesting looking Acoutrements for
smoking mass pot, and me with tartan
the bottom of Every pair
of Jeans that I owned.
The Rollers were beaten out of me.
I blame them for toughening me up.
Les Derek et al are entirely responsible for
the fact that Ive been Able to hold my own
Since 6th Grade. I had to fight the
Stoners, to defend their honour.
But ive never figured out how
I came to like them in the first
place how did I? how did I
Love something so Technically Naff that
I fought for it?

pg. 14
BAY CITY R
Les Les
THE
BAY CITY
ROLLERS!

OLLER
LES
EK
WOODY

we are not allowed to have
Pencils in our rooms here
but I snuk down a crayon
I am in Skipworth now
and Im going to Hillcrest
in a Couple weeks. but
after I go to Hillcrest
if I dont Fuck up I can
go back to the Farm
home. Well I drew you
a picture and I had to
finish it with my Crayon
it is starting to be
spring I can smell it
the Cherry blossoms
are so pretty. We went
outside a couple days.

ago and there was a
tree in the yard and
I picked a branch of
cherry blossoms. do
you know if my Mother
is Moving back here to
the U.S., I feel kinda
Nervous about writing
her. I dont know When
I get around her I
feel so awkword and
timid and weak and I
always find Myself
trying to prove to her
that I can make friends
and be popular even
though she lives on the
other side of the world.

Angel Dust

Falling like pearls from the mist
Shy we meet like lovers
you and I—
Our eyes are open. Our eyes are closed
Our closeness is something
nobody knows.
You possess me— I want you
And when I see fireworks I know
there's got to be something to this
cold hearted gloom
where everything's misty and grey
where I'm being pulled away
by the angels of time
the sparkles of life,
A spark that ignites the
silvery splinters of it all.
Time Life and space
are no longer relevant
and as our bodies meet in
this divine ~~[illegible]~~ haze of nothing
I see you are perfect in every
way and I feel as if the very
angels of heaven have
sprinkled the dust off their
Brilliant white wings onto our lips

written at the age of 9 about ? I don't think he had appeared yet. But he keeps on appearing & disappearing to this day

You remind me of someone
that I know
That doesn't know me
Someone who can fulfill my deepest need
That doesn't choose too
Someone that can tap the springs of my emotions
but won't
Someone as special as a diamond among glass
but doesn't care
Someone who I love
That doesn't love me
Someone who I need
That doesn't need me
Someone as warm as a summer breeze
but is always cold
Someone beautiful as an amber sunset
That doesn't see
Someone as brilliant as the starry sun
but cannot understand
my love

So excuse if I stare,
if my dreams flow through the air
Excuse me if I cry or get up and punch a wall
we're all only human, after all

written In Juvenile hall · Courtney dunit

Yea, We had the First Slumber Party in the history of Hillcrest Saturday. I swear to God, I was the Only one who stayed up til 5:30 am. It felt good seein' Saturday Night live, + Monty Python. Shit, that was fun.

♡ Monty Python night. I can do the funny voices. but I think Ill be a Rockstar. Get an Oscar too & Be best friends with Elton Jo

I live in this hole

(whorepaint, war paint) Well tonite
I got the Grop meeting and told
my life story and told about
Everything about how afraid I am
of not being accepted
(God! I cant spell any more) etc.
etc. and we have kitchen duty
5 hours a day so I dont Go to
School and Of course I bitched about
it stating to Cottage Supervisor that
under ORS. 169.83 (←?) it was Truancy
if under 15 you dindt attend
School. He laughed and told me to
call my lawyer and Now he
calls me his "Legal Beagle" SHIT!

I hate the Bleakness of this room,

the very walls are incarcerated and captured by the iron web.
gotta Get outta here
Baby whores wailing in a sacred unison.
nuns.
Daughters of Divine Charity.
that know no evil,
Rose milk from the porcelain breast all-to soon
turns to wrinkled homoginized yellow foam,

flowers from 1964 wilted remains in her heart,
Indian Batik and solid acrylic Turtlenecks not
tucked in. loose sex and whispers in the night
forbidden memories honored stored,

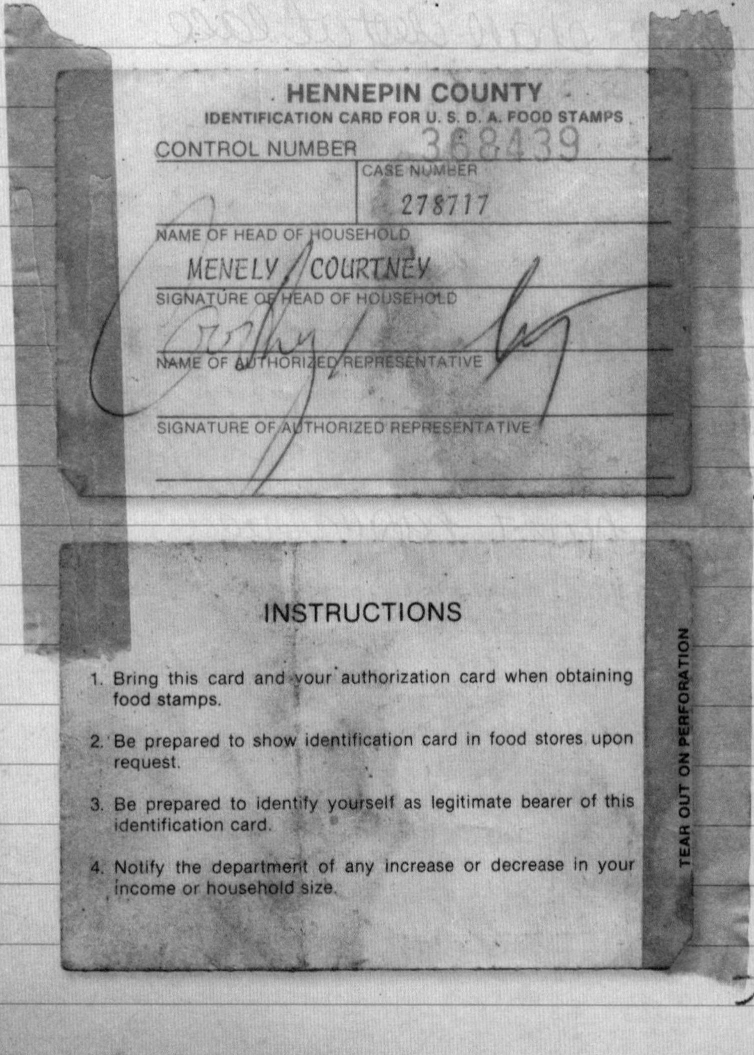

HENNEPIN COUNTY
IDENTIFICATION CARD FOR U. S. D. A. FOOD STAMPS
CONTROL NUMBER 368439
CASE NUMBER 278717
NAME OF HEAD OF HOUSEHOLD
MENELY / COURTNEY
SIGNATURE OF HEAD OF HOUSEHOLD
NAME OF AUTHORIZED REPRESENTATIVE
SIGNATURE OF AUTHORIZED REPRESENTATIVE

INSTRUCTIONS

1. Bring this card and your authorization card when obtaining food stamps.
2. Be prepared to show identification card in food stores upon request.
3. Be prepared to identify yourself as legitimate bearer of this identification card.
4. Notify the department of any increase or decrease in your income or household size.

TEAR OUT ON PERFORATION

death

and flowing money

and life in a mist
cutting dolls hair

This poem was rudely
interrupted by the world

I love my mother

This is Death Note no 43#

Last Will and Testament
When I die
Burn my Body
Take my ashes
Over the mountains
And the Seas
To the places I have lived
Sprinkle some
among the people I used to know
who I loved
and who loved me!
For there my soul shall rest at ease
let some linger in the breeze
Blowing them
to distant places
where my shadow
will hide all my
doubts + sorrows
leaving only
all the joys
my heart has carried

Quiet Room Status #1

HILLCREST SCHOOL
289-01-016A

31018-412

NAME: Courtney Menely-Kappa

DATE: 10-15-79

BY: P. Dillabough

WH: CENTRAL FILE
YL: DIRECTOR SOCIAL SERVICE-COUNSELOR
PK: ASS'T DIR. S.S.
GR: OTHER
GL: OTHER

EXPLANATION:

10[30]/pm Courtney awake and cooperative.

11[30]/pm Courtney finally sleeping.

1[00]/am Still asleep.

Courtney slept without any disturbance. She was checked throughout the night.

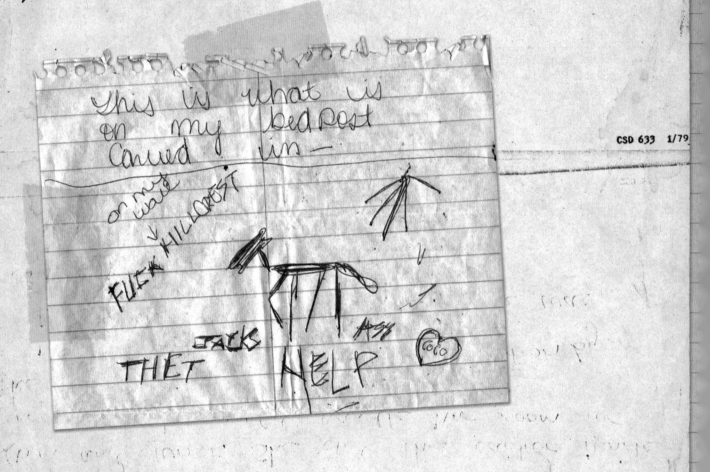

This is what is
on my bedpost
carved in –

on my wall
↓
FUCK HILLCREST

JACKS ASS
THET HELP
COCO

CSD 633 1/79

HILLCREST SCHOOL

Zeta Quiet Rm.

HILLCREST SCHOOL
289-01-016A

Quiet room report

SP*31019-412

NAME: Courtney Menely

DATE: 11-11-79

BY: A. Powell

WH: CENTRAL FILE
YL: DIRECTOR SOCIAL SERVICE-COUNSELOR
PK: ASS'T DIR. S.S.
CR: OTHER
GL: OTHER

EXPLANATION:

Courtney began screaming and swearing about bugs in her room at 11 ^{50}/P refused to be reasonable. She became louder and more insistent.

Coordinator was called and Courtney was escorted to Q.R. by Mr. Rommell, 1 male Zeta staff and myself.

She entered Q.R. at 12:23 A.M.

CSD 633

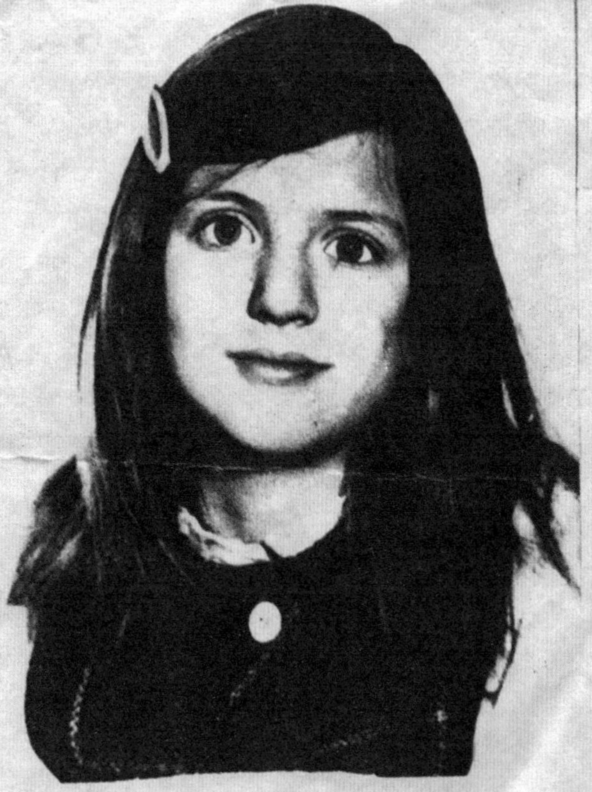

EDITORIAL

There is NO such Thing as Girl Love, Because all cool Girls are competive cunts, wich is worth loving in itself so its okay. Just dont pretend its otherwise. Celebrate the reality!

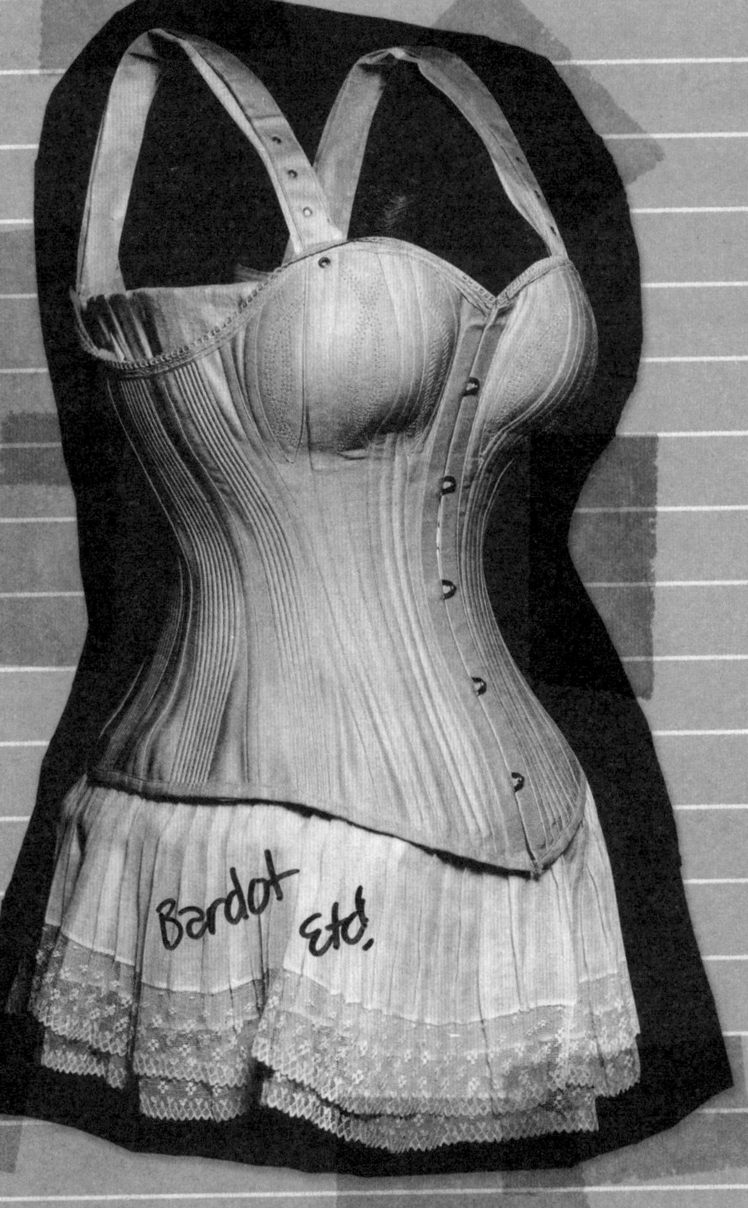
Bardot Etd.

my body is my temple and doesn't need to be abused by being sat in lye filled baths every day and using detergent and abestos on my hair (no less dye).
I want to be clean inside and out sparkling and pure.

It means parting with elaborate cosmetics. It hurts but its okay.

I dont have to part with my clothes except the wearing of stilleto heels constantly and tight pants that cut off my circulation

and underwire whale bone bras. I dont have to part with anything except some rituals - how worth it it will be.

Ive sat in this place
for 2 years,
had alot of pain,
Shed alot of tears,
played alot of games,
turned alot of pages,
But I cant beat the system,
nothing ever changes,
never seemed to worry whats wrong
whats right
Just seemed to worry
about who Im gonna fight.
Thought I was big stuff
impressing everyone,
But I learned the truth, I was recognized
by no one
Never seemed to care
about life in general,
But the heat started seeping through,
remember this is hell
and ever the hardest of us have to break.
Our soul is the only thing they cant
take.
But these walls have brought me
peace, tranquility,
And now I've learned.
I must love me.

HILLCREST SCHOOL OF OREGON
STUDENT REVIEW COMMITTEE REPORT January 30, 1980

CO: LANE PO: NEWBY DOB: 7/9/64 DOC: 3/27/78 KAPPA COTTAGE

MENELY, Courtney

REASON FOR HEARING:

Courtney is being seen by the Student Review Committee to be considered for placement. Courtney was last seen by the Committee on December 5, 1979, for a regular review.

ACADEMIC PROGRAM:

Courtney is enrolled as a full time student at Robert S. Farrell High School. She is presently in the tenth grade and in Mrs. Newton's core class in the mornings. Her afternoon classes include US History, drama, and studying in the Media Center.

Courtney's adjustment to the academic program at Robert S. Farrell has been excellent. She has maintained excellent grades throughout her entire stay at Hillcrest. Since Courtney arrived on Kappa Cottage in September, 1979, she has consistently done well academically. The previous school quarter which ended in November saw Courtney make honor roll status.

Behaviorwise, Courtney has had significant problems in the school program. She is a very intelligent young lady who tends to over extend herself as far as dealing with people in the school program. She is very outspoken and to the point of having or causing problems within the program because of her boisterous behavior. She has been sent back to the cottage on numerous occasions in the past months because of behavior problems in the school program.

Courtney's academic ability is seen to be far beyond the typical student at Hillcrest.

COTTAGE PROGRAM:

Courtney has been involved in the GGI program on Kappa Cottage since her arrival. There was an approximate six week session in which Courtney was removed from group because of her negative, hurtful behavior. This seemed to have a definite effect on Courtney and when she returned to the group program, she handled the help sessions in a much more positive fashion. Courtney's major problem areas seem to be her low self image. Courtney does not feel that she is as strong as she appears to be. She puts up a very good "front". While appearing to be very strong and capable externally, internally, Courtney appears to be a very frightened young lady who has never met with very much success at anything that she has tried.

Courtney has made some progress in the area of improving her self concept; however, her anger and hurtful behavior toward others is still evidenced on cottage. It seems that at times, Courtney spends more energy trying to find ways to beat the system rather than trying to work within its confines to accomplish her own goals. This behavior pattern has been consistent in both the Guided Group Interaction groups and on the cottage behavior. Courtney is presently expressing some very severe feelings of fear regarding placement in the community.

MEDICAL AND PSYCHIATRIC:

Courtney is presently in good physical health. She has been referred to Dr. Daly, consulting psychiatrist and has been seeing him.

pg. 30

MacLAREN SCHOOL

CHRONOLOGICAL DATA SHEET

NAME Menely, Courtney Michelle NUMBER 4659

#1 Visitor's Permit To #2

Date	Assignment	Home Visits
3/27/78	Zeta (reception)	5/25-5/29/79 Sally Johns
4/7/78	Theta	
11/7/78	Hilltop	
11/27/78	CCC	July 28 2006
2/9/79	Zeta	This is a
2/16/79	Theta	copy of all
5/25/79	FCTV	the places
5/29/79	Theta	I lived while
6-1-79	F.C.	In the Juvenile
6/12/79	Zeta	System. "Parents
7-19-79	a.a. Court hearing	whereabouts
7-20-79	F.C.	unknown"
8-14-79	U.A.	CLC
8-27-79	Zeta	
9-4-79	Kappa	
11-20-79	a.a.	
11-26-79	Kappa	
12-21-79	a.a.	
12-28-79	Kappa	
2-1-80	Foster Care	
2-6-80	U.A.	
2-21-80	FC	
3-17-80	ua	
4-9-80	Parole	
5-24-80	Termination	

Date Sent	Date Rec'd	Item
		Commitment Order
		Court Summary
		Birth Verification
		Public Welfare
		Other

Form #159
Rev. 3-74

C

Case Closed
5-24-80

VICTOR ATIYEH
GOVERNOR

Department of Human Resources

CHILDREN'S SERVICES DIVISION

Juvenile Parole and Community Services

2450 STRONG ROAD S.E., SALEM, OREGON 97310 PHONE 378-5289

PAROLE

COMMITMENT OFFENSE: .Theft II; Criminal Mischief II

PROGRAM: (Institution, Community Adjustment)

Courtney remained at Hillcrest approximately eight months before a first attempt at community placement was made. While at Hillcrest, Courtney displayed numerous personal problems in peer relationships, acceptance of authority, a low self-concept, and self-destructive tendencies. During her first institutional stay Courtney seemed to make some progress on improving her self concept and learning to cope with peers. She also learned to adjust to institutional life and appeared to be becoming somewhat dependent on the structured setting.

Attempts at community placements have been problematic. Courtney continued her former pattern of challenging adult authority, running away to avoid problems, and seeking immediate gratification of her needs. Further complicating the case is the fact that Courtney pushes for the freedoms of independent living while displaying many dependency needs and repeatedly asking for authorities to find her a "home." It is apparent that Courtney has been in search of the family life she has been deprived of for so many years and has rejected substitutes as unworthy.

Currently, Courtney has stabilized at least temporarily in a placement she found herself while on a runaway status in California. We are
awaiting an of ... have contacted
Courtney and t ... n, Echo Burgess,
is in her late ... ith autistic
children. She ... n-ager who is
related to her ... ccepted respon-
sibility for Co ... the home can
be licensed for

~~Arabia X Knighth Abyar Primitive~~ Zs16x

DROP This class
take challenge Exam next term

Dropwr121

Dublin

I hate Cheapcolleges – Sleazy universities like this one. Cheap Colleges have Cheap Staffs. You learn nothing you do Nothing Everything is Libaral, nothing is traditional.

Traditional Values are the Rudiments of learning— Repetition, Boredom etc. Combining Elements of "Games" and "Moderness" with learning is a Public Education way of trying to evade the inevitable, that learning is hard.

I find this Class an insult to my intelligence which isnt hysterical but does exist.

Nothing Should be Social Everything should be Covered with Ivy all the Teachers should have attended Oxford Courses should be Competitive —

me commenting that all teachers at a Juvenile hall should have been Educated at Oxford

whats left that isnt swept by the Rages of Apathy?
why do i always Crave change?
when will it settle?

oh Desire
oh money
oh Greed
oh

oh Accomplishment.

Eye me up for i am fuckallovalamiable
i am pretty and chunky and young.
i am Godless and Demanding nuerotic and
Gutsy i am sexual and Dreamy and
painfully Extraintraverted. i am
full of – Fantasy and lies and
astonishment and A Greed to hate
and A Greed to love and a Greed
to taste impossibility and a Greed
to Fuck.

Liverpool

Records

JD 12" – Transmission

Talkingheads – Fear of Music
Faust

Patti – Ethiopia/wave/Easter
Copen Pash Friend, Treason w/
Leonard Cohen (?)
Beethoven: 9
Greatest hits of Roxy
Sex Pistols/Bollocks
Bach (imperial canon – fugue ?)
Young Americans
Stage
Nutcracker suite
Siouxsie Greatest
Love (?)
Motown Compilation
Scottwalker Comp.
New Order
J.D.'s Greatest hits
Heaven up Here

Associates Club Country
Bauhaus – Kick in the Eye
E. B – Breaking the Back of Love
E B – Rescue
PiL –

Romeo Void
Nuggets 65 – 69
Marquee Moon

I desire a friend more than anything,
I desire a love, I desire safety –

me and ~~Rebecca~~ Robin after a sweaty lorry Ride its not English properness. we had a tape player and played Ride Loud Experimental punk perversion music in the LA Bus Depot Cafeteria - in our fringe punk Gear the Scouse boys with Greasy faces came and sat at our table. Scallie boys with no brains, when we breeze through a Council Estate we we see their roots. But were just poverty stricken transients of a different nature - el love those Scallie boys. Sunday morning at 6 am the only soul is a 17 year old Scallie boy hardened Criminal and his Blurry Dog. he invites us on a Robbery we decline delicately and he says "all ya have to do is Stand and watch. 500 Quid" no no no! we talk about the decline of punk the usefullness of life. he asks to walk with us a little way because the police are chasing him for no reason - we walk through squats Banged out windows and Greasy intact ones. the old Council Estate meets the new sturdy one. its like Liverpool meets manchester. Industrial severity meets Romantic filthy decadence. (where boys are Boys and Girls are Girls)

Dear Linda

for next year I've chosen to continue my Education here in Liverpool, enclosed is a copy of fees, what I need from you is a Financial guarantee Regarding living expenses. the course Im taking is a continuum of A levels (Considered Advanced Course).

Please note that an estimated living expense amount for twelve month stay in the UK not including course fee is around 5000 pounds – this means that what Im getting now comes to around half that amount not sufficient for a financial guarantee. In order to get my Visa Reiberated I need to have this guarantee, and a letter of acceptance from this college, they wont give me this until there is documentary Evidence of my financial state, and 25% of the tuition fee is recieved by the Registar.

So, please note the reccomendation on the General information sheet and let me know about your feeling on this. the $500 Im recieving now seems to have me at the bone and beyond seeing as that was thought up 2½ years ago, things have changed and Especially in Britain. (Im writing you pre crisis ← personal and maybe pre-war) national So, Regardless, I need the Documentation and also perhaps a few copies so I can send them to the Consulate and any major medical things that might come up

Im Doing fine and am Enjoying myself. the Band Im in has a imminent Recording deal so maybe Ill be so rich you wont have to even bother –

Love Courtney

Julian Cope &
c/o Peter DeFreitas
20 Devonshire Road
Liverpool 8,

or go to Dublin again & go to Trinity College
I want to major in
x Theology
x physics
x Drama

~~God you~~ should see it when an early clash song comes on in a Liverpool club all the lads are falling all over themselves yelling "We were there, at Erics the Riots, The Pistols we were THERE..." the only thing that outdoes that is when a Doors song comes on everyones up doing their ~~[illegible]~~ versions and its like okay Go back to sleep theres no place to go from here....
Ive never paid to much attention to Rebellion though, what with my mother ~~[illegible]~~ playing Crosby Stills and Nash and warming up the Hot Tub it would have been pretty STUPID. She was real into ~~[illegible]~~ punk though she didnt like the Nihilism just the tokenism, thats all it is now anyway, a bunch of my mother clones – late converters born to early late or whatever
So what if theres no MOVEMENT? no CAUSE? [illegible] wait for the next But its Going to be as shallow as the last Face it if you werent in on it in 77 your Going to have to wait 7 years and by that time youll be too old.

well you know there aint no Devil

If Liverpool was a person
i wouldnt sleep with it

theres just God when hes

its the cool of the Evenin and the sun Goin down
i want to hold you in my arms i want to put you around
i want to break your bottle, and still at all your charms
Come on Baby well set off out the [illegible] alarms goin down town
you Got to tell me Brave Captain
why are the wicked so strong
how do the Angels get to sleep
when the Devil leaves his Porchlight on
Lunton In Ireland. I think
I stole it. Dublin Bewleys. 1982

We learned now ya know I learned tonight
I have to make them love me. Ive learned
how a combination, never even
thought.... I didnt ever.... no
just in terms of my crushes oh not
even that.... How to make
Ghost he showed me how to keep his
even love me that all Baudelaires –
Abandon the slay them.... it
lost innocence Feminism is for the
old and sagging Idealists – I

KNOW HOW TO HAVE SLAVES! I know now... noone ever told me why didn't someone tell
me? Someone should have sat me down and said, Now ~~Courtney~~ Chrissie they should have looked at me
and fearlessly told me about how when,

I got older id have a power,
cause... have to
use it.

pg 40

cancelling all broken hearts forever, and
Ever amen, sorry lovers Im going
~~to~~ sleep and God forbid my soul
~~to~~ keep because when I die flesh
absolved Ill eat them whole Ill
love them all long and longing
Breast to Breast / Cheek to
Cheek.

Note here

years from now (I think of who looks and
years from now when I write)
I will look and chew when I first
learned about love.

I can't have
what i want. i never will. i want love nonstop and
Adulation for a million faces. a mother that loves me and a
father thats always there. friends and expression pure thought
and clean consciene steady stable erratic consistency with
plenty of room to breathe

Crunch! Crackle! Go → oh fuck off all of you

insidious is the word for this week

Sub word

Malignent

lastweek it was petulance + Baudelaire F.Scott Rose.Mary Rodgers and Kerouac

Everyone Copies Everyone here Mac copying Tom Verlaine who copied a fag French surrealist. Julie Coping ever deepthroat that Ever withstood the Gates of metaphysical ~~love~~. ~~luv~~. puppy luv, Deb Iyall copying Patti Smith who Copied everything that Ever impressed her Ever. I dont know whether to Respect it Envy it or hate it Because i cant find it in me to adulate anyone except those in immediacy. I love (pure personal level) Bunnymen Because its drawn on me seperate from Locool Consciousness but not altogether i cannot so crawling into it at all → I love Teardrop because of obvious but ive come to appreciate Both entities products in new wierd way ~~life~~ on an artistic plane instead of personilized theyre both my favourite Bands, Bunny first Because theyre more. I could see JC first if he was more realised and less a slave to himself heroes and defo <u>not</u> in love

thisweek is nowater

sheslostcontrol

Ideal Books

148 x 105mm (5¾ x 4⅛in): A6

Binding number	Ruling	Pages
411	Single cash	160
418	Feint	192

Soho London

Ideal *Index* Books

148 x 105mm (5¾ x 4⅛in): A6		
4141	Feint	160
4142	Feint	192
210 x 148mm (8¼ x 5⅞in): A5		
4146	Feint	160
4147	Feint	256
254 x 203mm (10 x 8in)		
4157	Feint	160
297 x 210mm (11¾ x 8¼in): A4		
4164/2	Feint	192
4164/3	Feint	288

27

Songs

I Wanna Be Evil - Eartha Kitt
Andys Chest - Lou Reed
Some Velvet Morning - Lee Hazelwood and Nancy Sinatra
Do the strand - Roxy Music
Girls From the Street - ?
Sweet Virginia - Rolling Stones
Lovie lovie - Kingsmen
Wild blood - Seeds
~~Beach is Burning - Venus And the Razorblades~~
~~Use Me - Julian Cope~~
~~the Disease - Echo~~
Never ~~forever~~ Say Never - Romeo Void
~~Big Brother - D Bowie~~

Beethoven 9 -
Bach - Imperial
All pianoforte -

Clothes
Big Protective and Dark
Desire
Relaxation
Books
the little Princess
the Secret Garden
Claudine at school

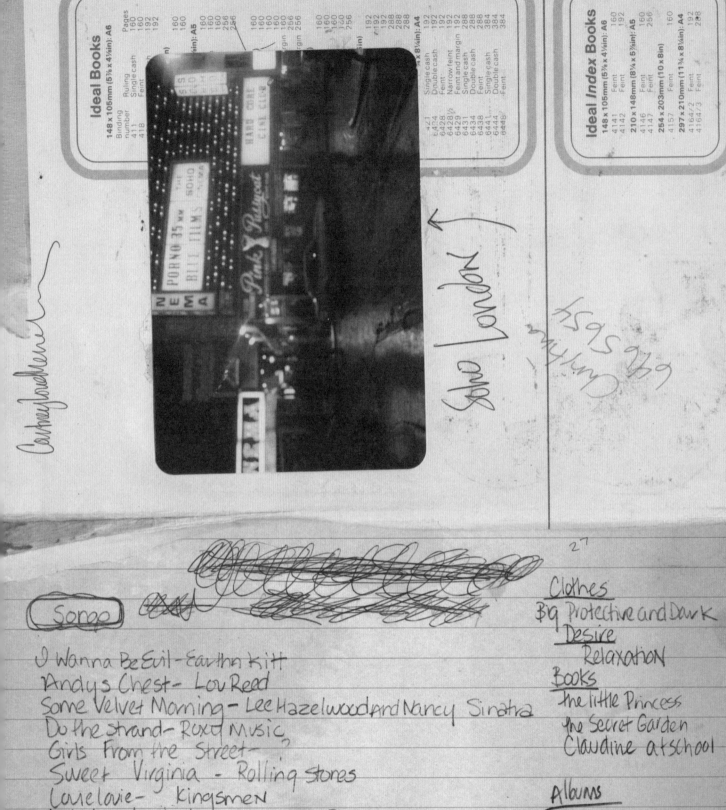

Albums

means the downfall is he tends to ostracise things
and alienate people because hes in love so tender
and its in love so strange, — so self,
and ungeneral thats as bad as macs morose
plodding and ungainly outrage but
it seems that theres more to relate to
perhaps its the macho man in us all
why do I find Ju so much more Challenging.
than Echo Macalloch? ← "Bore", yet I find EBMs
songSingsing more.... simply Enjoyable?

Repent

April 19th Nothing at all has happened today.

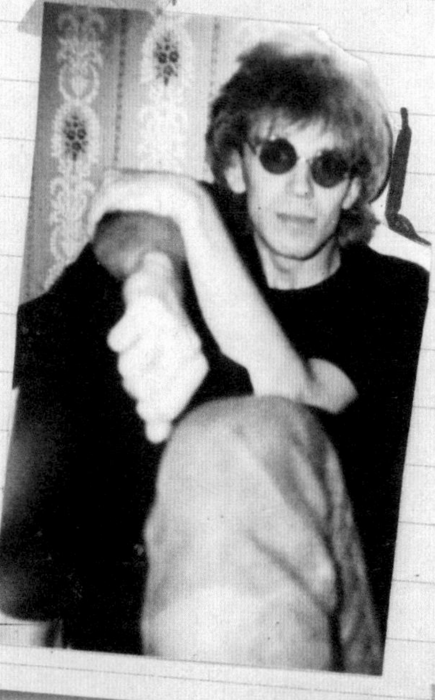

theonly2.

Shortened

Makes it right / loveclub

Star Trek
AA Milne - Kipling -
Milo
Daffodils
Halloween
"Young Americans" Bowie
~~Temptation's" ... ~~
Suzanne Leonard Cohen
She's lost Control Joy Division
~~Creem Magazine~~ - Tzers -
one of the *three*
Rogets cafe

Dance of the Sugarplum fairies
Methyl Dioxide
Shinjuku and [redacted] Roppongi
County Meath Ireland / County cork / Drogheda /
Rough seas (Bombed Saltwater ha haha)
One flew over the cuckoos nest
Fantastic life
A Good mouth
the lining inside my Gloves
my Daddy
my Daddys teeth and Discipline

I'm going to live in Ireland
someday *

Hatesquad

The Birthday party
Thumper and Bugs
Las Vegas
Bomp Records
Los Angeles
[redacted] Jim Morrison
- Ganje -
"Sound and vision"
K Marx
R Reagan
[redacted] Mopsy
The moral majority
The Icarus / Kiwi
| [redacted] C Anderson
school of superfold lyric writing
Red - Reds
Watership down
Easter

inasmuch as I fought it, I miss the routine of the institutions, both of them, one stricter harsher but altogether different — I feel the ultimate need to go back to the institutions to my parents they're the ones who taught me. you can't steal that I miss the institutions, I miss them. so what perversity motivates me to work with Juvenile Delinqueents in the very institution that held me? who would hire me on the Grounds that it's innate, it seems natural not Revengefull or Idealized, I know it, I understand them I have compassion yet perception of their whole view. I know to be as distant and remote or as overbearing and assertive as need be.

Quote

"the words vitriolic and diatribe should be changed to petulant and plump - [redacted] ribandd and senseless way, but you only here once." No no, Don't jump, implicid Don't jump shut my mouth before i say too much

July 21 1982 ,

here i am sitting in the Aeroport. Heathrow. Supassing 3 Liverpool Chapters. Sweeping them away Julian. Micheal. (see he won!) Bardiom Kevin Atmosphere Joy Division Echo and the fucking Bunnymen. Englishness. Goodbye. i can make tea now. i can remain Enigmatic pose well and appear feminine i can take many physical appearances risks as well as writing some of the Better lyrics around. Mark Smith is very Good. i can play music and understand technology. i can stay in and resist temptation too make the first move or stay too long or worse Get intense. American style. i have friends some of them perhaps lifelong. i wonder if i shall go to school , i miss the smell and the drive but i dread the Boredom. Dont talk to me about Cope we all know and if theres one thing i hate its Girls who Go on about the Love of their lifes breaking their weeping hearts. so everyone in Portland that cares to speculate may do say but mums the word on my side Babee because theres one Asset Everyone has until they spend it. their mystique. i do have some fantasies just old Remaining familiar favorites. about men. it would indeed be horrible to let them get the better of me. to let them have me. sweltering wet blustering Romance ! God i hate it and hope its just a phase. we are conditioned to believe that at one point we blossom and find love so i turn 18 and sit here opened mouth waiting . actually theres something quite lovely about Being 18. something wise. ill Go and call my mother, nono i wont, on the Bus we drove through, the tiny English midlands so lush so verdant i was given a lager to slosh in the Green nightness. we stopped and i had Egg and chips to be Really scouse. in the room the women come and Go maybe theres a hint of Michelangelo. its time for a new book.

AD 7535759
Fluers Du Mal
Fluers Du Mal
Fluers Du Mal
Jules Verne
Fluers Du Mal
Fluers Du Mal
Rikki Tikki Tavi
San Francisco
San Francisco
San Francisco
153 miles to SF San Francisco

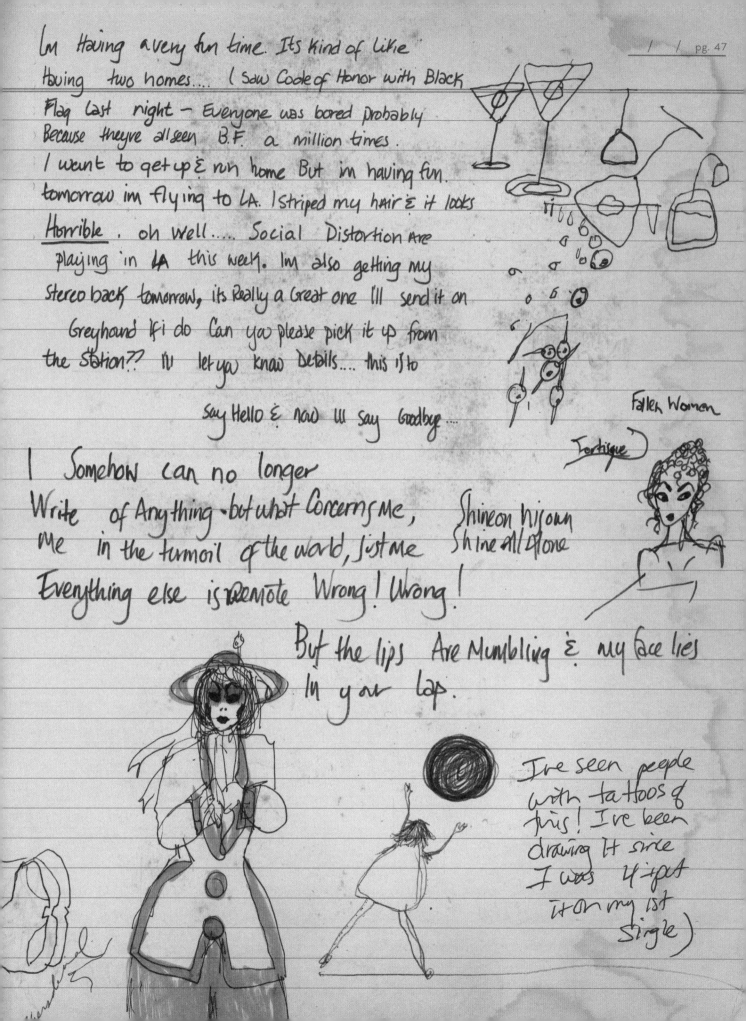

Im Having a very fun time. Its kind of likie Having two homes.... I saw Code of Honor with Black Flag last night – Everyone was bored probably Because theyre all seen B.F. a million times. I want to get up & run home But im having fun. tomorrow im flying to LA. I striped my hair & it looks **Horrible**. oh well..... Social Distortion Are playing in LA this week. Im also getting my Stereo back tomorrow, its Really a Great one I'll send it on Greyhound If i do Can you please pick it up from the station?? I'll let you know Details.... this is to

say Hello & now I'll say Goodbye....

I Somehow can no longer
Write of Anything – but what Concerns me,
me in the turmoil of the world, just me
Everything else is remote Wrong! Wrong!

Shine on his own
Shine all Alone

But the lips Are Mumbling & my face lies
In your lap.

I've seen people with tattoos of this! I've been drawing It since I was 4 (put It on my 1st single)

my last European Evening: MoonBathing
in the Cot in Paris its full and it
Feels me. I do want my hair green
Again But Ive got to get a Job,
oh Paula, you Beautiful Monster were
Got a strange Trek ahead of us...
Im not stopping, unabashed assault on
Creativity, no Plan B about it,
I am Born first of Purity, and
Secondly & most important of
desperation - I must make this Quickly

This Jumping from the Ocean in the
Night This Emerging from Trees
Rupert Everett Star of our Video

Nanana Plague is about This Violation
& this Ideal Pain. oh yes, I am
Exemplery of the Rockdream ladies &
Gentlemen I give to you
Provencal Portland Oregon

Beggars Banquet

Sharon Jones
"its a good table for you too"

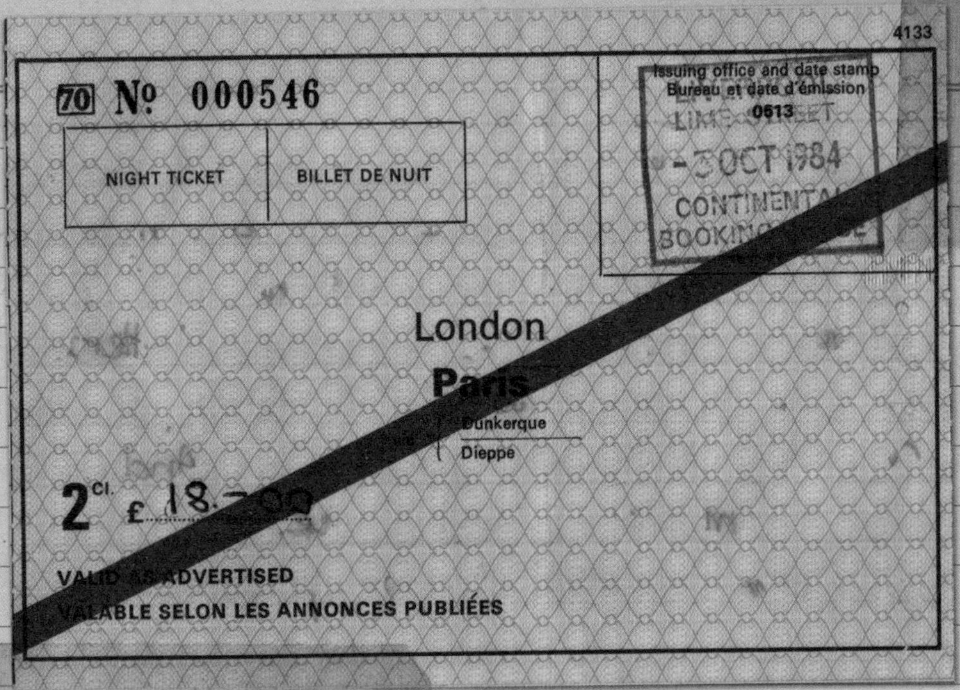

4133

70 № 000546

NIGHT TICKET | BILLET DE NUIT

Issuing office and date stamp
Bureau et date d'émission
0613
LIME STREET
- 3 OCT 1984
CONTINENTAL
BOOKING OFFICE

London
Paris
Dunkerque
Dieppe

2^cl. £ 18.00

VALID AS ADVERTISED
VALABLE SELON LES ANNONCES PUBLIÉES

i changed my mine.

i think Roddy Frame & Richard Butler are Possibly the two most Gorgeous men Alive. Roddy Frame is Because im so Envious. when i was 15 I wanted to do what he did and hes a thousand times less Jaded. Richard Butler Because he is just him. A Stupid SouthEnder homely as sin who is Crass and mellowed by America.

One day Ill write loads of songs again. its my only Hope.

I am 20 years old.

I am not a Beautiful youth. Adolescent Boy.
This Experiment in Boyishness has Failed
I am a woman... MAYBE I am a women
I depend upon Artifice As I have been Taught.

I ♥ SIMON LE BON
I AM A DURANNIE
I WILL BE
SWAN
SWAN
SWAN
Feint

well there now thats the End of Europe - for awhile
my mind is filled with Crazy daydreams

of selfish inward
things like
cows hoses
moonlit hells
of old lace
& Arsenic,
Mickey &
Rock Bardin.
Roddy Frame &
Johnny Marr
Slim Pop Gods
me and
Pk Visial
in the snow
Dickens in
America -
Nanana
Plague.

RIMBAUD

keep the Rose, the Civilization,
the Direction words
like swain
O wisdom! Young Master

its
will be
st
de

March 21, 1985

I must stop smoking soon. I __must__ stop
smoking soon. you die of smoking
i must choose to die. __when__ i choose.
i cannot die of cancer
its quite frightening to Be a
smoker i must look so cool
im sure i am
you sweetly langourous
ethereal in my arms
Apartheid is definitly my pet peeve
Vero Beacht
Oh swell he said, he said
and it all sounds the same to you—
Right? write....
whatll become of me & the way i eat?
so lame!
so lame!
im no spring chicken, though
theoretically i should be.

AVOID POMPOSITY
LIKE TH

the only real love i have Ever felt
was for Children & other woman
Everything else was lust pity selfhatred
lust
now Look Again at the Face of
Botticelli's Venus,
kal, The Judith of
Chartres with her
so called smile
then i am
Burning all of you
in Testimony.
Laugh!

PLAGUE

Yes. I have a Rage for Success
A flame that i dont always
pay attention too.
my house on the Corner of
Egomania and humility.
i moved to the Corner of Rich & famous
Then to the
lovely ~~Estab~~ of PROSPEROUS & ACCLAIMED.

a quote from "Lifestyles of the Rich & famous"

i will never pine for power
i only need to be
taken care of and touch
people. lots of them. And then in
turn take Care of Everyone
and have
truly Great Kids.
As long As im Fertile.
i dont think its fair
if i die. But it will be
okay if i do. Just
desolate,

Apr 1885

Its notlike im Actually
ON THE STREET just misplaced
dis GRACED disjointed.
and a little Bit Betrayed
yeah a little Fucking Bit
BETRAYED okay? so im dressing
uptonight. "Jingly Jangly Guitars
paisley & lace & dreamy Sensitivy"
Oh God! Give me a Break.
did i forget to mention
"last years Funkadelic sound"? Naw
could i forget that pray tell.
Yes Robin lets Comission someone
to make us silk suits.

Gone into a Garden. There was a subtle
sigh in her throat. She has taken on
too much. Groan Groan Groan. Pet White
light. Sometimes i think its All a
slow singe. Ive Got no determination.
Like they all say im a fucking
whirl a Big Mess that Keats
would have died for. i was
Born intolerant.

full of Ghosts.
That intervene. with a wierd
star. a wierd twisted intense
wavy fatal glow that wrapped
around me like my search
for perfect dependance, Blue with
choking on this umbilical.
Ah, she said. Im ALONE. Ach Na.
Fuck Me, i laughed Guilty
at a past prime.

1. Stuff a room full of Lilacs
2. Aidan Quinn & Judd Nelson
3. Horse in "80"
4. moonbathe 30 pounds less
5. Stop Smoking
6. Amadeus Soundtrack
7. Stuff my face into Lilacs

Clean Clean Clean
Clean damm
living

& sometimes shed just cry these
Enormous Masturbatory
Crocodile tears over "her Lost Kat"
or ~~[illegible]~~ "My Micheal" or Get
Terribly Fishey About this one
"my Jeff" shed say &
Collapse. She rarely drank—
She said America was just this
Country addicted to Sugar Alchohol &
tobacco. She was like Gloria Swanson
about the Sugar and the Red meat
as well.

{ I am not here as a muse for those
Revolting old Ghosts from my Pasts. }

I hold onto beauty—
Practise my makeup & my pliets
living just to die for another day
ill whirl & dance & die in your Eyes
ill fall into your arms
I need you so simply.
I need you— just must find
that Beauty
Somewhere.

The language
of love

is the
same

as

letters

Suicide notes

Wedsday

i like kat shes cute. shes
got very good taste. shes strong.
shes Talented
she wont call her Parents
for Money & she wont work.
So what? so just what
am I supposed to do.
my job situation is slow
But it will work out. i pay
the rent. what About
Everything.
I understand her not
wanting a sleazoid
job neither do I.
But still.....

July 10

I never said I hated England. My House is Fab. Very Big.
Very Roomy full of space. It's worth alot to
me to pay this much money sucks & I hate
Thinking about it. I Love Daddy so much.
also dont care about
who I love.

Pola
Negri

well what
About Ambition
I dont know if
I trust kat.
She makes me feel immoral.
i am not immoral & so
what if it looks like i am
This is my home, and hers.
Eat: Fuck it...
i am happy

Frances / Girl
CLARE
Wich name?

Things to teach my
Children
(i will have four children.)

Frances
Clare
Scarlett
Kevin

never let anyone see you beself promoting : stephen

stay a Virgin. Sex is Gross and should only b accomponied with Equal love. ← until at least 18 get a horse Instead

Be a brilliant equistrienne

never smoke

film directing is far better than film acting

Get Enough sleep

fantastic wardrobe

play & work, but NEVER BE BORED

Be glamarous, get your high lights done every 16 days

Be honest. Food is for peasants. but dont get rexy. learn the ways of the English & the French

pay Even the littlest things Back. never borrow any money anyway. I'll Give it to them

Pray

Earn your own fame.

KEEP YOUR

Clare/Frances you will be very spoilt. dont Abuse it

Clare
→ Dont trust my taste in men but if i ever really fell in love with someone other than your dad you'll know because I'll not have 3

We shall live in
Beverly Hills
English Countryside
New York
London / Ireland
Provence /

Dont take taxis.
Keep your Enigma
DRINKING is DROLL
write letters vs. PHONE
Nighttime is best
Learning is fun. knowledge is a Quest
Summer & hot Places are a Curse.
always be creative.
Alchohol & cigarettes are weaknesses.
Disgusting ones. Dont
have weak flesh.
enunciate
Dance well.
Be humble
Be Faustic (dry)
Be Quiet
Dont Fight. if you do WIN.
If you lose Ill fight for you
Reading is a Really Good thing – its departure from Squalor.
Food is for peasants
Go to College – oxford.
INNOCENCE
Think About Boarding school only in the UK

Dont spend money too fast
Keep disiplined in what the training is for.
Be obediant it will be Best noone will be asked to do that much.

The blues are nice, but dont be led around by the Blues.

Tea & hotties & Edward the Bear & Milo & Dublin & Liverpool & pastels Grey muted reds, blues, & Books & fun camp & Laura Ashley & Lilacs & tarot & Astrology & Vegetables & Apples & natural hair & face is all okay, but highlights are okay too.
DONT SMOKE. Acupuncture
Coffee Electric blankets & smurfs & Hersheys & LA & Chicago & Red & Neon & Video Games & biteless new things & peer pressure & pot & Gold & God & Cults & Red meat & twinkies & makeup & developed sexuality is all
WRONG.

She will always have Spectacular Birthday parties

~~Qeeit~~ Room

into the Quietroom
where the lullabies are kept
& childrencome & cry at night
~~& cruel stars turn into scars~~, noones ~~sleeps here~~ where ~~ever slept~~

& ~~why~~ do i deserve the
ice of isolation
protectmefrom But lead me to.
your Final destination:

Faith is all we have here

where did you fall
why did you Run
why am i alone in here
why am i alone

shoved into this Qeeit room
full of ~~phantom ships~~ deceits
& shattered ~~love~~ youth lies on the floor
& all your ~~feeling~~ hearts in Bits
~~where do we go on the Honeymoon~~
~~The eye of the~~
all into the Quiet room
now theres the Great divide
& twilight Brings you hearing all
the Babies Locked inside

here i am in the eye of the hurricane
or where do we Go on the Honeymoon
in to the Quiet room

a taste of exposure wont throw me into a whack, i hope not. i dont want to talk about it. Just my perception gets so lazy & full of Avarice Thou art free, But thou art Fickle. Byrons lazylidded contesses. Byrons Ariel Boring Byron. what a fucking image! Burning :: my throat for Caroll Baker. for Baby Doll. for candy & magazines and sateen hats.

REM. Gingham

has;

1. saved me from Being a perpetual ANGLOPHILE forever.

Awful song

i dont know?

Killer forgot your Alive

Lawrence oliviers famous face. My
Larry! Vivien! Vivien!
my Bands songs are going through my
head. Voice lessons, Voice lessons!
wormer with Babooshka shaking
a stick at me.
obscene * doesnt go 1. and it
doesnt go 1-2. it
GOES 1-2-3

Nancy studies.

Alba 77

1. Evil smile
2. punk Rock Queen pose
3. "Wake up sid"
4. Pensive thoughtful & pretty & psychotic
5. Fat ugly & strung out

Torrid. infantile. warped.

Best Sunday dress

(intro)

E { Terrified of the corruption hear the thump of each Breath
x4 { i am Going to i am Going to & am Going to live through this.

A { i am Sleeping in the River
x2 { drowning in the Blue moon

E { i Run away from all the messes
x2 { & leave each Bridge in a state of Ruin
Bass x4 Swim on your side, we will be perfect Again
was so much cold

*A { x2 there
all the light poured out of you

E { these things that Go unsaid
x2 { just Burn down houses that's all (they do)

A C E { & i put on my Best Sunday
x4 { Dress
& i walk straight thru
mess of

i put on my bitch Boots
into the fire

E { Terrified of the corruption
x4 { & so afraid of the disease
it couldn't be you with innocence
or me with Bravery

A { no more infections from your friends
x2 { no more seizures by the sea

E x2 { i walk this clay
like a lullaby

A { & noone throws Rocks at me
x2 { & noone throws Rocks at me

E { you can have your pound of flesh
x2 { just x2 justify it

A C E { x4

Repeat twice

I need money so I need a job. im hopeless at Everything But Children. Autistic or very small. i look too scary.

Its the night Before the audition its 3am.
wish me luck.
i am Nancy.
Dear God i think i can do This.

Late August night. Los Angeles. im up so late. its so the same here. miles of hell. funny wierdness – Got up in the morning & rolled into a pool. miles of money....

ACTING

- GET ALL PARTS OF 'LK' GLUED ONTO ONE DEMO VIDEO
- GET JOAN'S 8x10's –
- TYPE RESUME
- SEND OUT TO LA & NYC AGENCIES.
- LOSE LOTS OF WEIGHT

i stand Everyone up Romantic Tragic & not so dammed Skinny at all. i need makeup. most of all i need Nancy & fame.

i love Jennifer Finch much. Im Glad shes realizing herself – so unapathetic. little temptress. IM owned by her spirit – no i dont think ill ever have too much Bad to say about her Talents, or her mind.

Truth & Passion those things you can never put down.

LIVERPOOL

Laird studios →

Velma was Great fun for me.
it was a huge challenge in
that it depended on me
Not ~~[illegible]~~ getting heavy
and watching alot of CARTOONS
and just overdoing Everything.

i didnt have to think like an adult
i didnt Even want to.

Kats been here not
Quite 2 months
Weve written 4 songs
'I see Nothing'
'Colder than me'
'My Angels'
Next is Gonna Be called
'All roads lead to'
Weve played 3 times.
had 2 Bass players
heard ourselves on
the radio w/out
Asking 4 times...

Everyones holding his Breath
waiting for Alex's next
MASTERPIECE and he hasnt
Even had one MASTERPIECE
yes, meanwhile, if you Cant
appreciate that in this Age of
Cinema, in a world of shit hes a
Directors Director as opposed
to studio fodder - It took
him ALOT OF BALLS to
Go make this Movie and his
to take the piss out of hissey if your CAREER
hip jaded cynical, your gonna
hate it. The First time i
Went to Blue Velvet in N.Y.
i was in this horrible Hip
Audience who were
laughing and murmering Before
the insect closeups,
Anticipating them. they
But to be honest it does
truly suck.

Do you now?
i have Been so small
around you & so alone
i feel my Bones aching
towards a new obssession—
Maybe this one'll be CONSUMMATED—
The obsessions old But the
hunt is new.

Knew they were SUPPOSED to
ADORE David Lynches
return to his INTEGRITY
and they Did. Id much Rather
GO out to A council
pub in Liverpool or Downtown
newyork then Go Do
Coke & Get in Free to Clubs
with people who Cant even
PLAY like who have No
SENSE of AKD TACTILE humor.

when you lose the Animal in yourself
your just a USELESS FAG PARTY
FIXTURE who is Gonna hate me.
who probably hates messy obnoxious
Kids and unhousetrained Dogs and
was never REALLY punk.

LOVE is
pheonix cat scratch.

Love is
you.

its not Enough.
i need a Connection
i need a charge.
its so lazy— to just get a fix of
LOVEGLUTTON

DARK shadows & Long Bones under
the skin of your face.
did you GLARE At me.
did you LOVE me.

the little Girls understand
Everything ANYWAY. i was the First
kid on my Block to have a
Fall Record ~~and~~ But i ~~would~~ was
Secretly obsessed with John Taylor.
Finally im Able to be true.
If you cant be immature
then your lame. youve Got to
Throw a TV out the Window
Sometimes — Especially now that
you cant Fuck or Do Drugs,
This is just ~~Alex~~'s TV out
our
the Window. its A Beastie
Movie. its for KIDS.
Fuck OFF — its COOL

My Goals are to Always feel
Brilliant About what i do. to
have CHRISTMAS Every DAY.
EveryDay. to Gain so much
DENSITY and BRILLIANCE that
as an Actress i can Find
SPIRITUAL ENLIGHTENMENT.
to Afford A really creative
M~~ake~~ Aid, to Dissappear when
i want to And to
Never Give in to Boredom
to have Every Day Heaven and
christmas and WORK

Jean

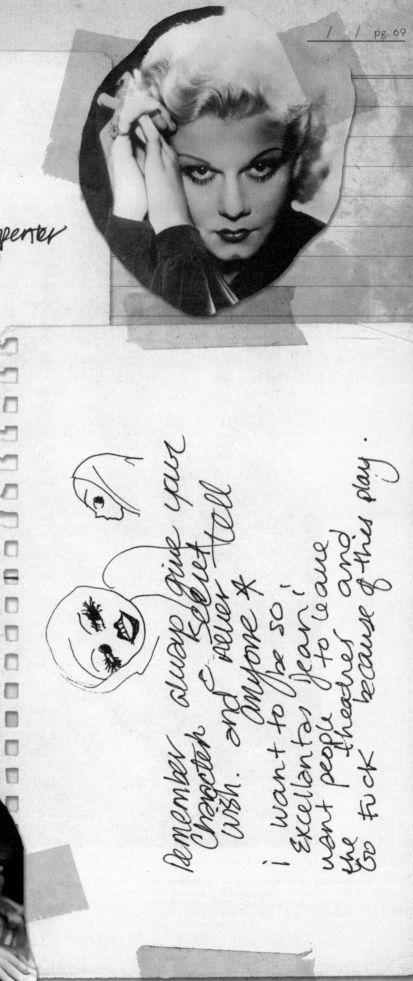

b. 1911, Harlean Carpenter
Kansas City Missouri
Dad; Dentist

Girlschool

10 yrs. moved to LA

Extra work. / opposition

Hells Angels

Perfect Example of
how you create illusion

ILLUSION

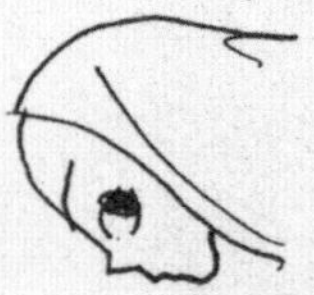

Remember always give your
Character a secret
wish. and never tell
anyone *

i want to be so
Excellent as Jean;
want people to leave
the theatres and
Go fuck because of this play.

Producer: ERIC FELLNER. who ~~love~~ hates me. one day I'll get my nose fixed & Gain his Respect. Sara Sugarman. Kathy Burke. I know this film sucks & I'm not pretty (yet) but I will succeed as an actor. just not for this.

PHOTO CREDIT: TOM COLLINS

Alex Cox & me sleep under the stars. we do not fuck.

Cusack came for the day, oooh my I'll *never* tell

"STRAIGHT TO HELL"

ISLAND PICTURES

Courtney Love is Velma, the moll of the gang, in Alex Cox's raucous action comedy "Straight to Hell," an Island Pictures release.

STH4

Testament to my Charisma *not* my face. I'm getting my nose fixed ASAP.

Ladies do *not* kiss & tell.
Tim Robbins: a bit pretentous

COURTNEY LOVE

THEATRE

Ashland Oregon: attended Shakespeare "camp" at Shakespeare festival 6 years.

Talking With (Handler)
Storefront Theatre,
Portland, Oregon

After the Fall (Maggie)
Portland Civic Theatre,
Portland Oregon

Marat Sade (Charlotte Corday)
Portland Civic Theatre
Portland, Oregon

FILM

SID & NANCY (Gretchen)
Directed by Alex Cox, 1986

STRAIGHT TO HELL (Velma)
Directed by Alex Cox, 1986

MUSIC

Faith No More /Slash/ Epic Recording Artists)
Singer & Guitarist

Ive Been locking my doors
for the devils and the Ghosts
and the Shadows that i cast
when i Ached the most
and the parade marches on
they are looking for me
But they'll never find
the one that you see
Im the Girl in the doorway in
the Rain and i know that
you'll come back to me Again

Since ive chanted my hairs grown
ive lost weight im confronting deep
seated fears, and i have a career.

Once i was walking in
the West Village and i felt
transported Back to the
sixties and it was gorgeous
and i wanted to make love
but there was noone there.
so i walked with my friend
Arthur to Times Square
with a broken shoe and
saw a horror film.
Halloween came to New
York in 1986 and i was
the UGLIEST GIRL IN THE
WORLD i felt like Genet in
a cell full of my own shit.
instead i was at A ROCK
party ~~At~~ the palladium.

4/14/87

the proceedings went smoothly
for a Nightmare.

You fidgeted with your fancy dress and
your shoes were too shiny
As bad Actresses stole your
parts in Exotic locales, lying
in what could have been
your juiciest truth.
LIGHTS ON
AND NO APOLOGIES
im sick of parquet floors
and Good cheese
im bored with my taste in music
im sick of your Nostrils
& indulgence
i hate that your so fucking
Grown up & clean
Big ugly industry Ego.
Busy crazy Murder madmen
Lucky Girls flashy Eyes
weeping glitter drains and
blue kisses

April 22

i dont feel free sometimes
my Buddhism is my
freedom

Am i ugly i wonder to my
Lovers.
do they care at that
point.
am i really ugly?

Not, according to the television.

There are some true pains on this
Earth, there is some true
Hunger ~~someich~~ suffering.

i wonder About Blakes soul?

he was on a Graffiti Binge in
San Francisco. he wrote 'Sex is
Revenge' in every conceivable
place in the town. Every coffeehouse
toilet. 80 feet high on
trendy club fronts and walgreens.
Someone countered him
with 'Love is Revenge',
(Eventually i won by crossing
that out and writing
my own name as revenge)
i was leaving a lovers
house (one i want to
forget really terribly)
it was night on a backstreet
in North Beach and
the new Beat revolution
was occuring

the next time i saw c. i was
About to be famous and i was
98 drugs was in New York
and i had coffee with
him and his friend.
my head was screwed on
all wrong and I was in
a Rubber dress. i was
poor and confused but
my future was bright.

The Next time i saw C.
she worked at a trendy club
in New York. i was Brilliant
at a party. in New York i am
certainly Celebutante Status
and i had had my
Rockstars and my Buddhism
and my intellect was
Burning and returning.
i can hardly stand
Bleached Blonde anymore
its like Gunk i wanted
my English Major Blood to Boil.
'Call me,' he said so i did.
i saw him tonight and
i had tea with him hes
very impressed that im
Becoming a movie star
Well, its not going to happen for
many Real time years.
& I'll be a Rockstar first. I hope
when I get Famous to not be too
misunderstood. I've always gotten the men
I want & I have a premonition that
a man will somehow get me in hot water.
We went & fucked at his Apt. one day
I wont be so promiscous.... I really Wont

and so he should be. he asked
me how the publicity revenge
was Going. i said i was
over it. he handed me a sheaf
of Stories hed written –
one of wich i starred in
he called me ugly Three times
in it.
im Glad he thought i was ugly.
Because hes seen the Magazines
and he knows im a Blonde fox
"Starlet" now. the Fucking went fairly
well. I decided he was a little masochist.
& used my skills, learned in Japan & at the
Dominatrix palace to humiliate him. Ill never
Fuck him again. I didnt take his number
more than 3 blocks before I threw it away.
I think For my lifetime Ill only be In
Love max 3 times. Its fun to fuck.
But Im like a Guy. I dont want any emotion
or commitment from 90% of them.
I certainly didnt cum. Coz I didnt want to.
he will be talking about that blowjob for
the rest of his days. ha. as i stated
Ill never fuck him again.

Joni Mitchells on and i only love Bobdylan and im Back with leonard cohen and i love Ezra pound and kevin thunter now and im playing Jean Harlow in my first play and im off to London weesday to do the ll and covers of the Magazines.
and clay will write many more Stories

ica mueller
invites ya
to Go
"STRAIGHT TO HELL"
with
Courtney LOVE
IN
alex cox's
new film due out
June 12
SPECIAL PERFORMANCES
By pogues
& sex Gods

im in because if yadve Been inside someone and they rise and they Become famous you feel responsible in Some small way. or large way. and clay is not a Bad writer hes just a little Sad and i think he falls in love with probably lame cynical Girls.

DO NOT COMPROMISE

I must withdraw from those who threaten my integrity –

INTEGRITY

OR

INDULGE IN ANYTHING UNDERHANDED

BE

UNSWERVINGLY SELF DISCIPLINED

Liverpool was special but people there have not Aged or changed in five years. they just have worse Drug problems

i stand apart in liverpool.

the Columbia – the piano – harlows on Barstools

How i need to feel alive. how proud they are of me now.

your perfect Lord Byron
pulled you in him
Violently cringing
at the Glorious sun
of your flesh of one and
your heart a beast
and you killed him in cold blood
when he Expected it least
Perfect Lord Byrons
Gone Mad Again
he tells you that you
Are his passionate friend
he tells you that you Are the
Moth
& he is the flame
and when he fucks you Again
it feels just the same
as heaven flooding
Avalanche crying soul
beat nightmare
your Perfect Lord Byron
crushed and curled
his fist at the breast
of ten other girls
and then he walks home
alone in Terrific long strides
when the stars scream
~~Perfection~~ your name
thats when he died

all im saying is that it isnt wrong to want this masculinity its traditional & commonly to need to Serve Someone. its the role of the BRIDE. MOTHER DIVORCEE battered old bitch drinking Scotch in LA Afternoon She beats her children she fucks strangers. the pool cleaner.

— i saw Tim Roth last night, hes short but hes Beautiful. i saw Gatsby, Mick, etc. (Rockwives too, Jason.) but Tim Roth. Hes SHORT but hes FAB. like INTENSE. like I WANNA WORK with him. i did AUTISTIC as he CHECKED ME OUT. And then i DREAMED! i DREAMED i cut my tattoo off and Gave it To HIM. i hope he COMES

Dennis Hopper told my publicist i was 'very funny and a very Good Actress.' my Day was in the Bag. i Adore that man... XX

and Divinity

and why? why?
because love is DIVINE.

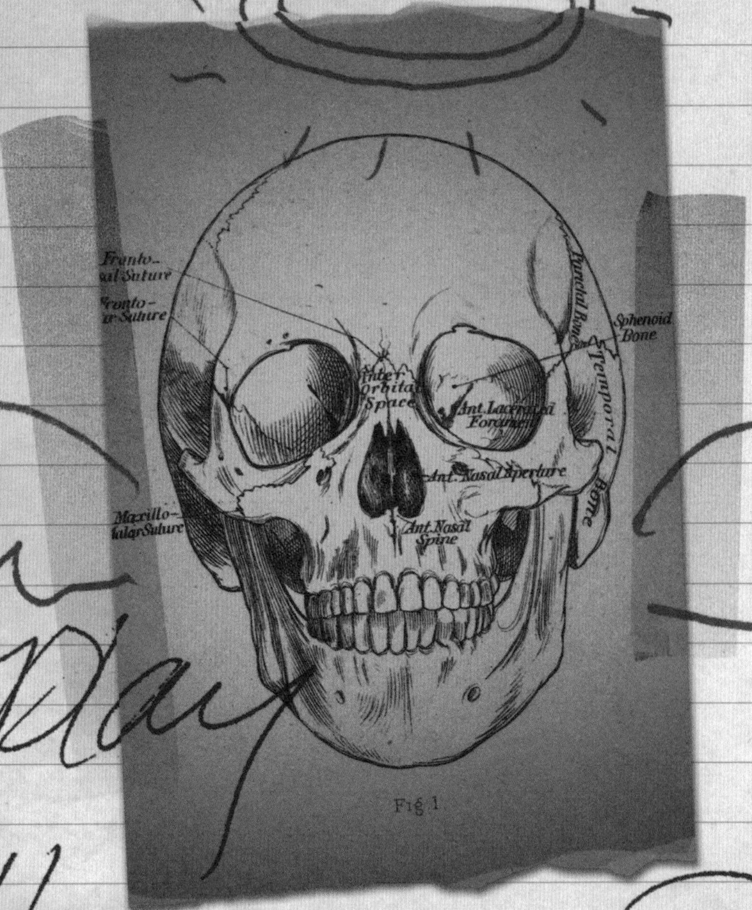

lets play

HIDE THE SKELETON.

SPRING
Compositions
Name Candy goes
School to the
Grade Midwest
9¾ in. x 7½ in.
100 Leaves
No. 77925
$1.49
Roaring Spring / Top Scholar Roaring Spring, Pa. - 16673

cold and ugly velocity
burns like cheap fuel
and who would startle this one with Love?
they would leave her there forever
battling her mad visions
and empty prophecies
Tipping thick LiqeuR and hardcore
Tunafish,
i cant live in this
I said picking up the Ashtray
its Not the maggots, crotchrot OR
smell.
No its the Abscence of hope —
It is by no means the
money that i owe — my dear —
it is the cold grey day that never
ends,
No, its the moments crying into
moments —
the satire of a life.

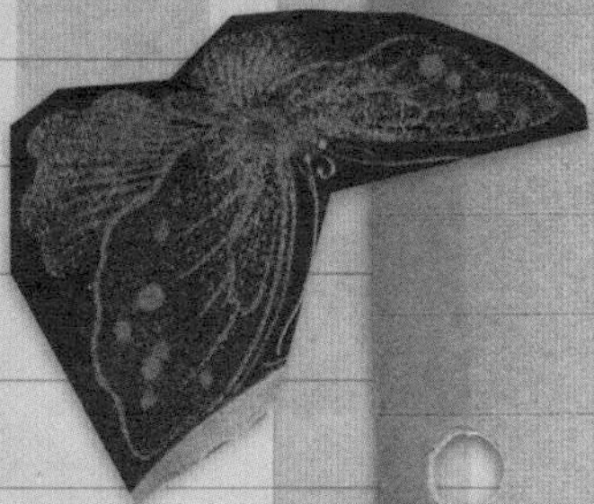

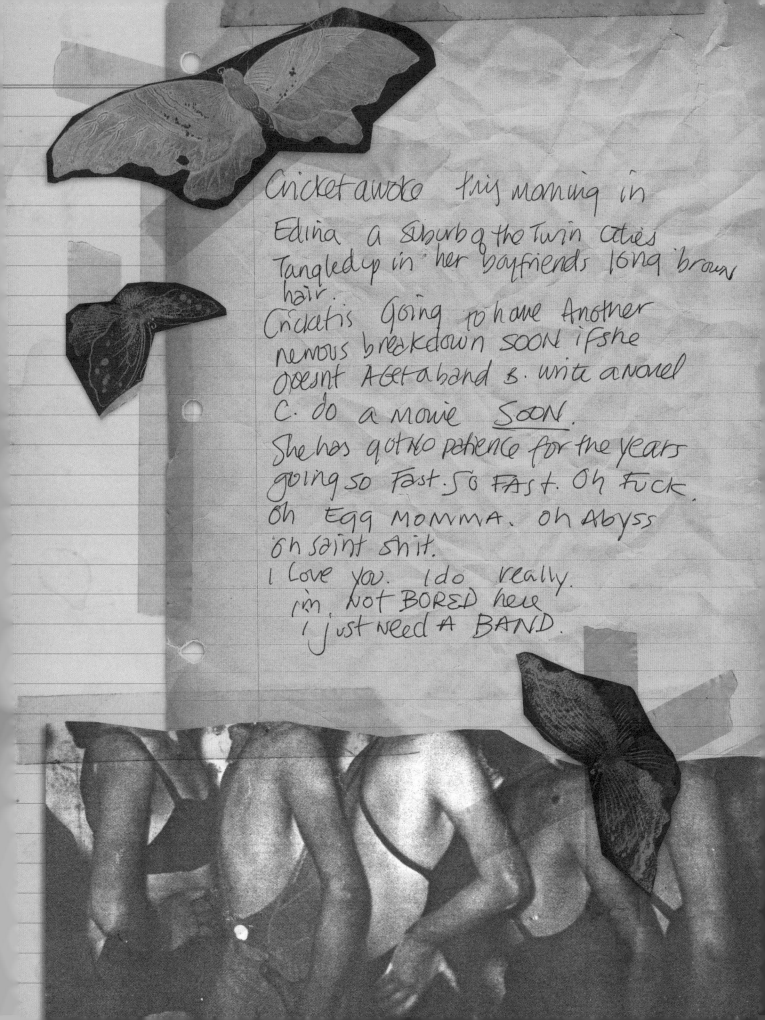

Cricket awoke this morning in
Edina a suburb of the Twin Cities
Tangled up in her boyfriends long brown
hair.

Cricket is Going to have Another
nervous breakdown SOON if she
doesnt A Get a band B. write a novel
C. do a movie <u>SOON</u>.

She has got NO patience for the years
going so Fast. SO FAST. Oh Fuck.
Oh Egg MOMMA. Oh Abyss
Oh saint shit.

I Love you. I do really.
i'm NOT BORED here
i just need A BAND.

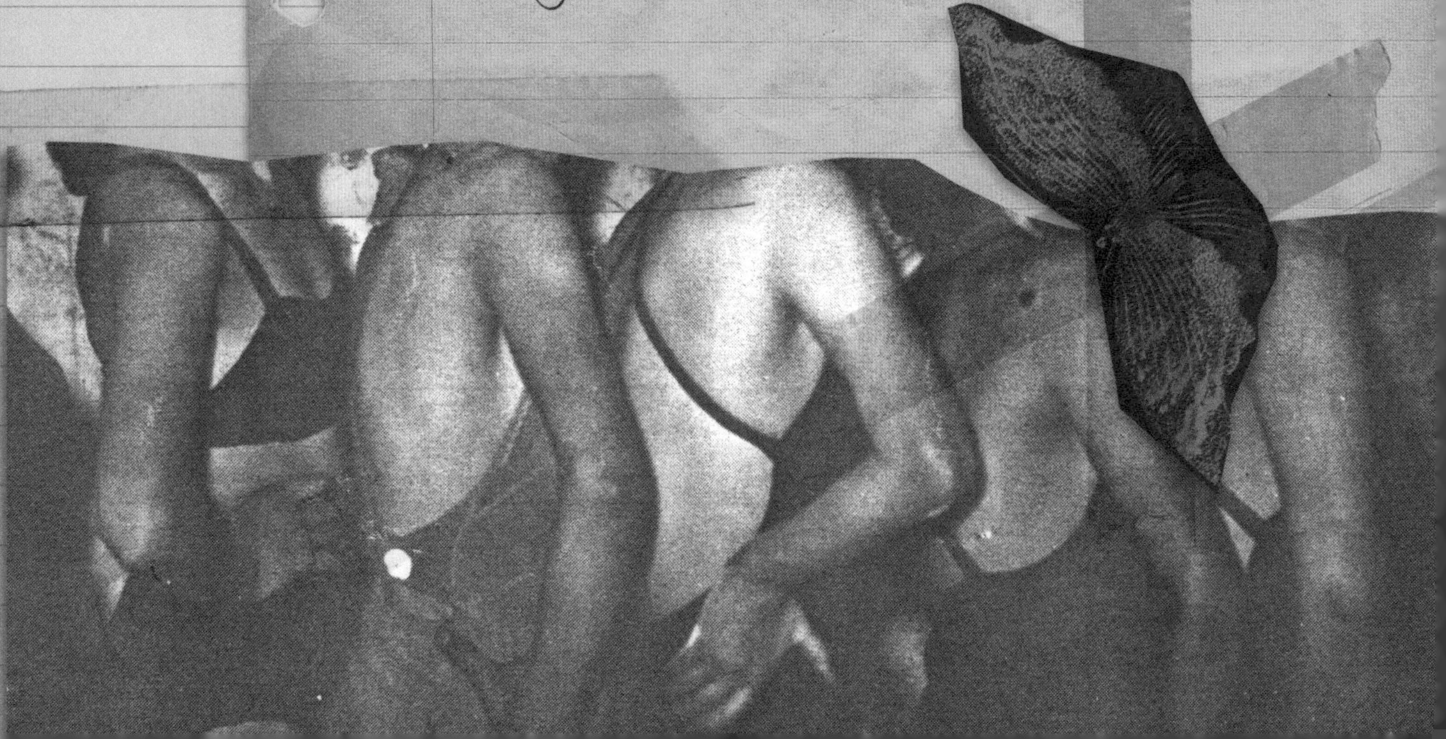

"God i, really hate intense
Conversations in Bars" says ivan
with little pearly teeth. Gnash
Gnash/ Gnash/Gnash pick that sweater
,baby. No big thing a tiny bony little groovy

I look
for the holy Fuck.

in Everything i see

Walking the streets
like a Lullaby
And whos throwing rocks at me

looking for the Holy Fuck
the psychic stripper
the mystic cow
the swamp pussy
all the
time
NOW.

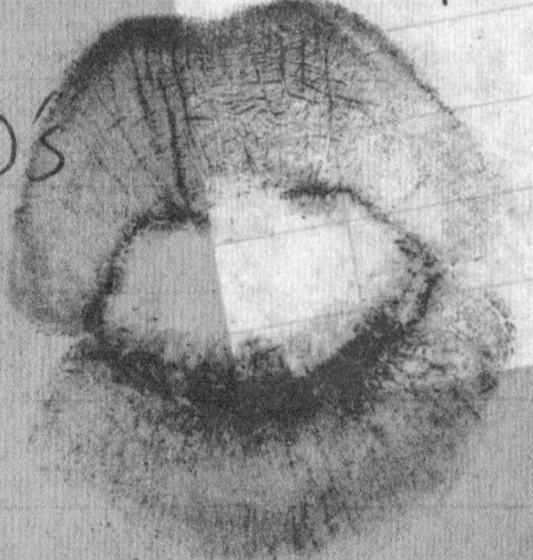

Cans of codeine
line the shelves
of the Gold shadows
again,
there is as well
a tide,
a fucking big black moon
on the June Bride
She hides Behind the veil
and forsakes her
Cool Love,
Yeah Fuck your
Confidence and oatmeal.
hypocrisy in a botticelli seashell
Sally were you the one
in the garden
my teenage
Season in hell?

thing, like the girl we go out with.
all boys go out with tiny bony things
And then im the Variety im the too intense
for words bitch, then they climb the
fucken walls, then they split and
climb onto the teensy weensy tiny boney
baby bee bee bodies in the teensy beddy byes.

May 5 -

i havent been writing much at all, this being Because ive been
so in Love. its springtime in minnesota and im beginning to
feel the universe is maybe malevelont, impersonal.
i dont like it here at the bottom, in the underside of the
wheel of fortune and i need some reassurance that im still a lucky
judicious special person, Able to have abundance.

The Orpheum was a crazy fucking disaster which i
DID handle with lots of panache. i love high stress,
power, whow, zoom. but its not so fun when it leads to
financial panic & trouble. Lori and i are barely on
speaking terms. ive moved from Amandas into Loris
and my Big lovely ready to fix up house. filling it with
Lilacs. ill be 24 And its No rationale to compare my
life to others Around me the same Age And think im ok.
im Not. Cant play the Hollywood game, havent got a
band together yet.
need a band by
next year. or Ill kill
myself. or end up
doing monty python voices
for a living... wich
would make me a comedian.
wich i never want ever to be.

Eyes will follow and you ≈ will follow
Eyes can come

& Eyes communion grate
divinity is it possible & you
Eyes – i'm too terrife yed
of them to look into
my heart Any MORE

Decoradive AN icing
nothing more
like BABIES

eye

SWEET CRYSTAL
POWERED
BY GOD

DICKNAIL
CLOUDS

Dear the right Guy at 4Ad,

This is our band Hole. we have 3 Guitars. Jill ar bass player played in Sylvia Juncosa And Super Heroines me, i started Babes in Toyland with my Friend Kat and even used to be the Singer in Faith No More wich is a Fairly cheesy thing to go Around boasting About but i really will do just About anything For us to get a Good old Fashioned color seperation LP ON a Nice FIRM label like yourself's wich includes boasting (apparently) about cheesy things.

Maybe you'll really like our single all on its own and say 'All Right you Girls Go make a Record' and you wont hold it Against me that i used our Ex bands to get a leg up. or down, actually in the case of the one ex "band, but im only telling you this to get ahead.

all Right man.

C. Love-Hole
& all Holes.

pg. 92

Dear John Peel:

Thanks for your interest in our band.
were gotten tons of letters because of yor show,
we will be putting out a 7 inch in
August and an LP by November
on Johns Label sympathy.

For some Background info – i came to San Francisco from Portland, Ore. and ended up being the singer for Faith No More for About a year but i was just a teenager and i dont remember it much, this was previous to thier Macho phase. then i met this Cool girl Kat and we moved to Minneapolis and started bands eventually being Babes in Toyland. Then i met this film guy Alex cox and did this pretty dumb movie and then i moved here and started Hole with Jill Emery who was in Sylvia Juncosa and an LA punk band Super Heroines, and Eric whos just sort of a Genius and Caroline our drummer, and we just got this New Guy Errol so NOW we have 3 Guitars, were really hoping to Get Over there to your Land soon and we would Love to do sessions for you i hope its possible sometime.

please let us know what U think.
thanks Courtney Love-Hole and all Holes! in General.

Dear John Peel...

thank you very much for
YS note here is all we
have we are Doing another
record for Sympathy and a
Subpopsinglesclub Thing*
we all come from LA
except me i come from
Portland, Oregon and
it is really really HOT
here right now so i wish
i wasnt here. we hope to
somehow come there
in the future –

OK COOL MAN
we will send U
stuff.....

Courtney from HOLE.

Beauty. Cant ever really believe
cose i generally find it corny and

process for me feeling sometimes an
woman it is at that point
of the Beauty

in female beauty unless its absolulate, i wich distasteful as in the case of Tuetonic

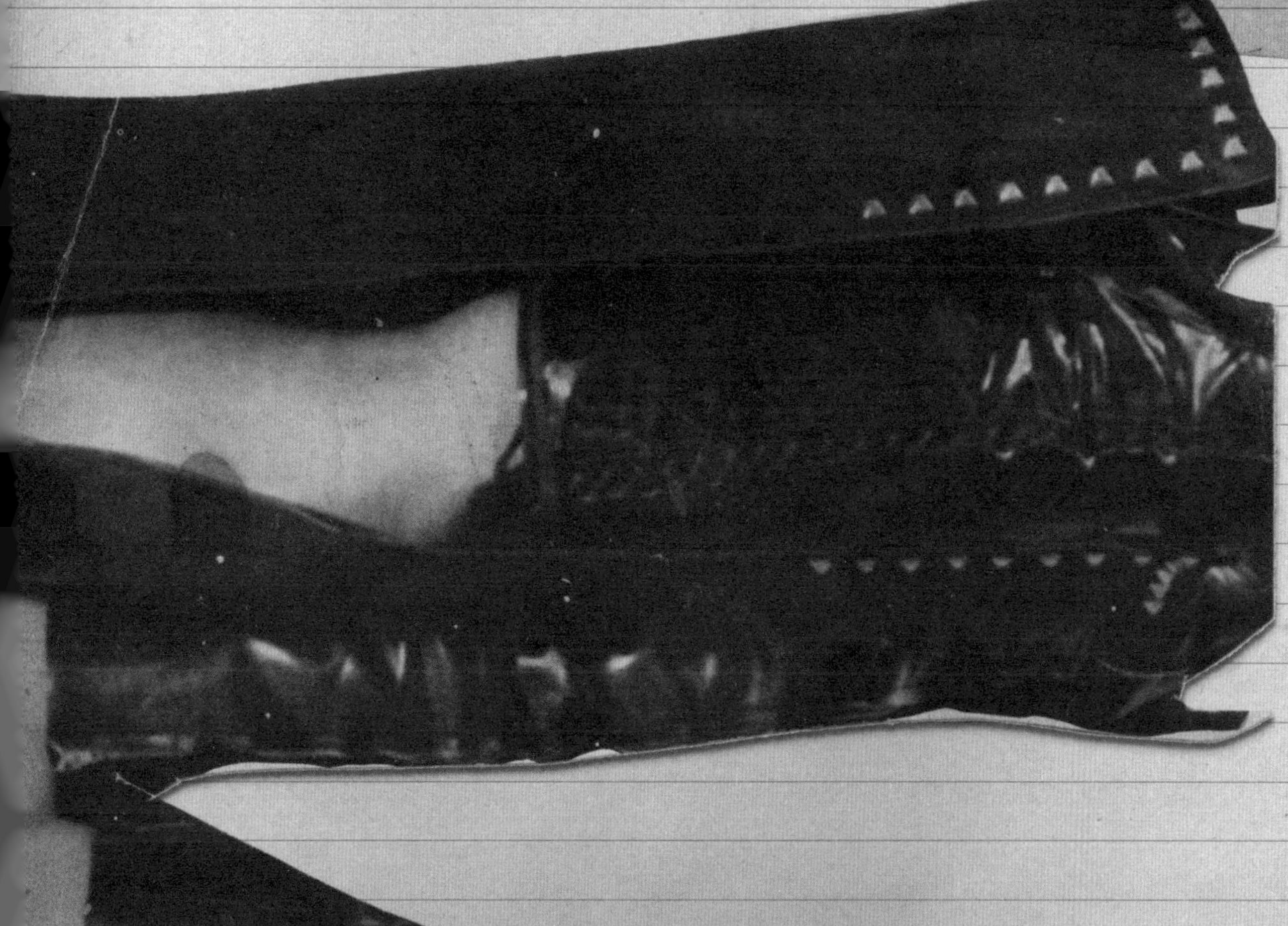

thick lipped blonde models, when i am finally and utterly convinced of a womens

beauty wich is an endless now in the presence of the

im utterly bored

When MAN finds GOD. As it were he has been picked clean: he is a skeleton: one must burrow into Life again in order to put on Flesh: The word must become Flesh: the soul thirsts. on whatever crumb my eye fastens i will pounce and Devour: Heretofore i have been trying to save my precious hide: trying to preserve the few pieces of meat that hid my bones: i am done with that. i have reached the limits of Endurance i can Retreat No further my back is to the wall. If i am a Hyena i am a Lean and hungry one. I go forth to FATTEN MYSELF H Miller.
FUCK
KILL
Some OK Bands
FRIDAY
AUG 24th
GENIUSES
cool
EXTREMISTS
REVOLUTION
CLAW HAMMER
and
HOLE
Tear its heart out
Shut it up.
AT Shamrock

LIVE ON THE SUN

the HOTTEST

GLAM FAG Bands this side of Eagle Rock.

L7 &

from Boston LEMONHEADS &

from the Midwest GOD BULLIES

& HOLE

EVERY SECOND 584 million tons of Hydrogen are being converted thru Nuclear processes into 580 million tons of Helium, by our own sun!

the ROXY WED NOV 21

∞ 8 p.m. ∞

Mother may I, set fire to the Sun,
my worlds so small,
My worlds so small,

Black berry tangle,
Blood dripping down
me, they threw a rock
at me, on Roosevelt street,
Mother may I, may I, tear out
thier ~~[illegible]~~, eyes
leave em in the Black- berry
Bushes. to die,

YOU, FUCKEN, SPIDER.

Ive got to be A blonde Again
with my mouth sucked on this
is miserable. I cant see life as a
Frump its just too HORRID
just talked to NYC [illegible]
Boring, ~~[illegible]~~

Salmonilla baby eyes & syphlistic
SACRIFICE.
My water breaks like Turpentine
Baby got waffen red lashes
and the Absent Carcass a vicious S.S.
Superstar Carcass out here on
the turnpike, you dont care if she says yes
Galaxy waving frantically
slit yr sky open and let the Moons
out yr throat

im A monster
Got a revved up teenage head
a real monster
California Born & Bread

MOONS & JUNES & FERRISWHEELS
the DIZZY DANCING way U feel
When EVERY Fairy tale cums Real
ive looked at CLOUDS
That Way
You cant Fuck
like me, so
Dont Even TRY.
L7
HOLE
SUBPOP BAND.
AFGHANWIGS
THURSDAY
JULY 26
AJ!S
Cracker Jack

HA!
"Whilst we . . . . . the conventional . . . . . were wasting our time on education, agitation and organization, some independent genius has taken the matter in hand. . . . ."
George Bernard Shaw
AFRSCAN
DODECAHEDRON
ICOSIHEDRON
OCTOHEDRON
SATVRNI
IOVIS
MARTIS
SOLIS
VENERIS
MERCVRII
LVNÆ

Spirit House
HOLE
Show starts at 10 + ×
Sunday × June 17th ×
LECTISTERNIUM ×
9300 W. JEFFERSON BLVD.
AT THE COVER GIRL CLUB
5$
/ / pg. 101

inviolate rose Enfold me in my Hour of Hours
Faroff, most secret &
chest, the sevenfold Gash in Heaven.
sleep that Porno sleep miss mousy.
and Everything but sleep
CINNAMON GIRL
Porn Star's $80 Million a Year
Can't Buy Tea With the Queen
THE
SONIC YOUTH
LIVE
AND
HOLE
THURSDAY
NOV 1
WHISKEY AU
GO-GO

~~I~~ I've since revised this statement.

6'3 +

Eric Erlandson
William Butler Yeats
Nick Cave
Thurston Moore
Neil Young

All Hot MEN
Are tall.

All Hot WOMEN
Are short

MADONNA, KAT,
KIM GORDON,
I AM TALL.

Blood Blister
Scar Tissue
Sell down
the River,
'Sister,'
Rue the Day
Give me Back
my water
spirit

Carnage, the sensuous truth of destruction.
wizards
&
HOLE
SAT MARCH 24th
Drunken Withered Manzanita Sisters
Late Snow
JaBBerjaw 3711 PICO

youve got to come to xpect this Thurston

baby, now that your a youthquaking
tastemaker,
now that you've put the "Be Cool or die"
Law into effect. I will ignore your Law.
& will not thank you in my Oscar Speech.
wich I <u>shall</u> have
the unsolicited
postal product, our hole 7,

all For you delicate as
little rosebuds, a fukin Machination
like licking the stamp, there you
Go, From us to you,
Love.
a Strapping healthy
young Bitch Goddess
from Blackberry thorn crawling
Oregon & the rest of em.
Let em all bunch a, chan,

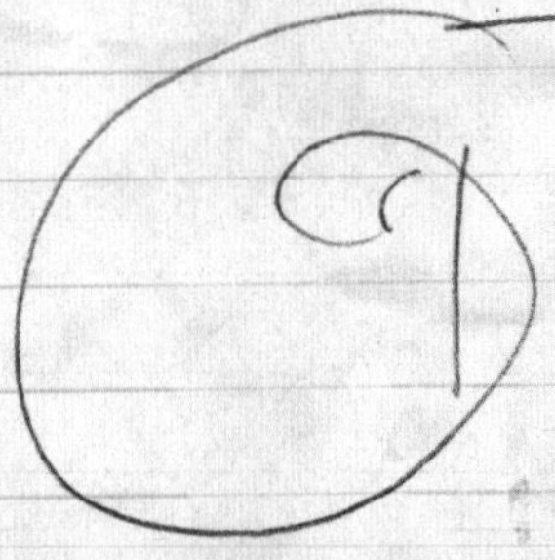

ELUCIDATE

Cant sleep. keep getting Lured from it by Messy Complex
Layersand Masses of thoughts center of the Matrix being
my band and the occasional twinge of Bad conscience.
my band and Thirst and Hunger for some sort of Everything.
Glory. maybe. But Also Freedom. Whole scenarios of people
revisited (Cathing my ~~[scribbled out]~~ soul loves) Competition with my
Friends Making all the Right Moves dealing with my
Lugubrious and semi alluring semi humiliating past incarnations
as everything from Liverpool whipping post to Sugar chigger
to Kat Bjelland to Roddy Bottum.
to Now how my dearest Nearest little Tuetonic
sweetheart lies wrappedin warm blankets in his lovely american
bed on a warm LA Night and im wanting it all
and that what its really all About im too old
right now to really want to lay it on the line, when those
Smooth hands wrap round me i just feel Right i dont feel
Bored or Frenzied just happy to be in the here and now
and when someone says Something Against him
i want them Banished from the Light.
i dont think K stole me. i just

think i gave her the Traditional Blueprint
For what A Fucked up Girl should be.
think that i sort of contributed and
help to shape that blueprint. it has Always Existed of
course. Girls should Generally be Loud and Fucked up or
i usually dont talk to them. Except if they are Quiet and
Fucked up in wich case they are even better in some
ways.

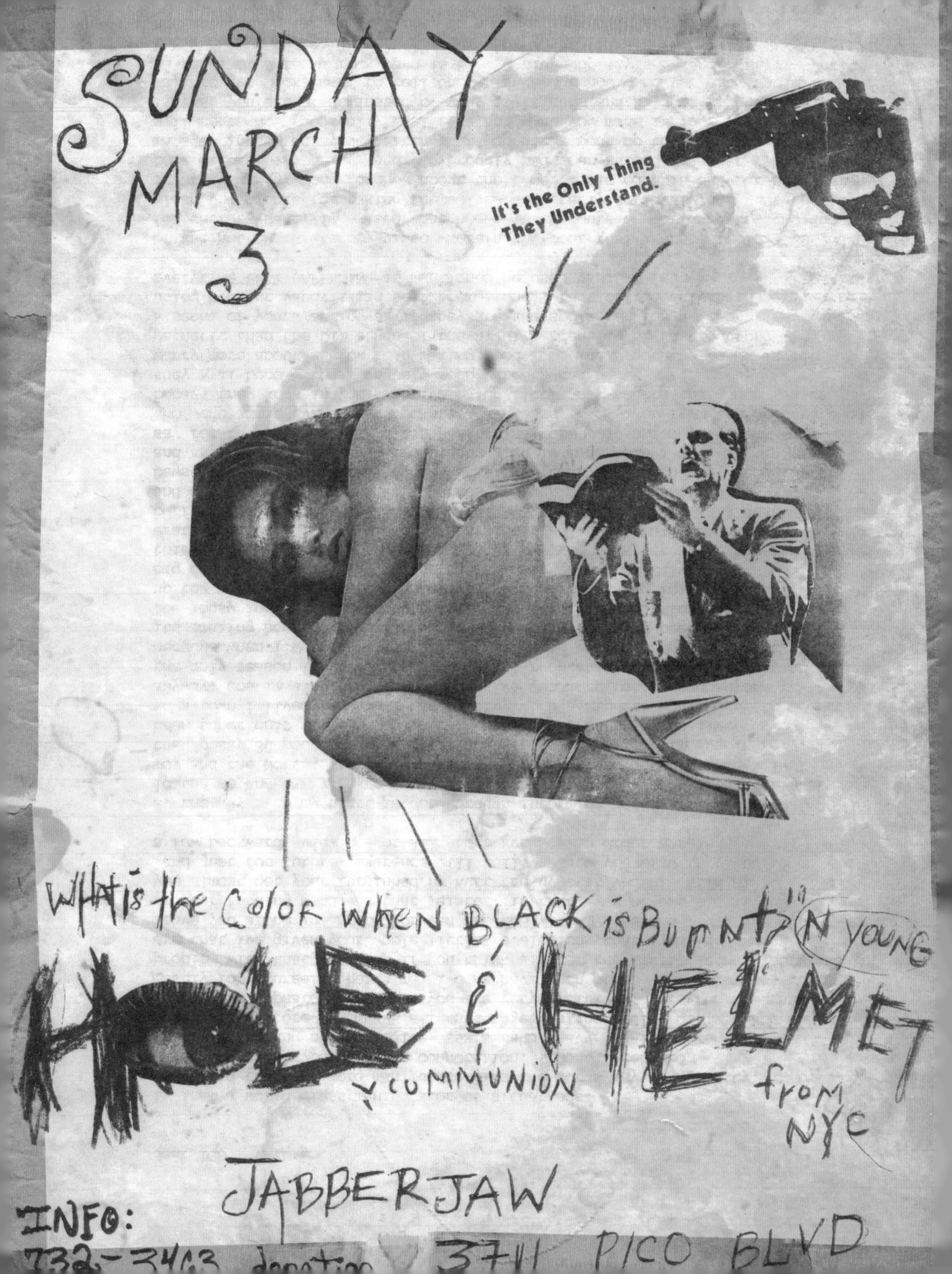
SUNDAY
MARCH
3
It's the Only Thing
They Understand.
what is the color when black is burnt in young
HOLE & HELMET
communion
from NYC
JABBERJAW
INFO:
732-3463 donation
3711 PICO BLVD

Pretty on the Inside

Teenage whore

~~bury~~

Good ~~sister~~ ~~BAD~~ SISTER

Garbadge

Clouds

Dicknail

Burnblack

retard

phone bill

~~LOADED~~

witch Finder General

Demonologist

Badfinger

SLENCH

SLOT

Wierd red Light

TEENAGE WHORE

BURY ME

WIERD RED LIGHT

Sugarheart

~~New ONE~~

MUD

2

Pretty from the BACK

GOODSISTER

something ~~FAST~~

GARBADGE

CLOUDS

MRS JONES

GAG

Turpentine

BLACKVIRGIN

Angeldust

NOSE

Taking it in taking it All in. it is truly
Glorious- Life - i want to Live it well,
i want to Help, The ugly the Disavowed
the Disowned the Terminal.
now, ~~my pla~~ i have NO patience for those
that would try, Though marked and
obviously outcast, i have NO patience for
them that deny their difference.
The only ones im interested in saving
(unbuddhist as it may be) are those that
are Lost and need to make a stand.
oh spring, winter, fall, Glorious
Summer now i am one of the
pretty ones and i vow to use it
WELL i will Never again
Scapegoat anyone - i will
~~help~~ them. God Bless this
Life i have Loved it and
will Love it even More.

man i most want to sleep with ♥ ; WB YEATS ♥

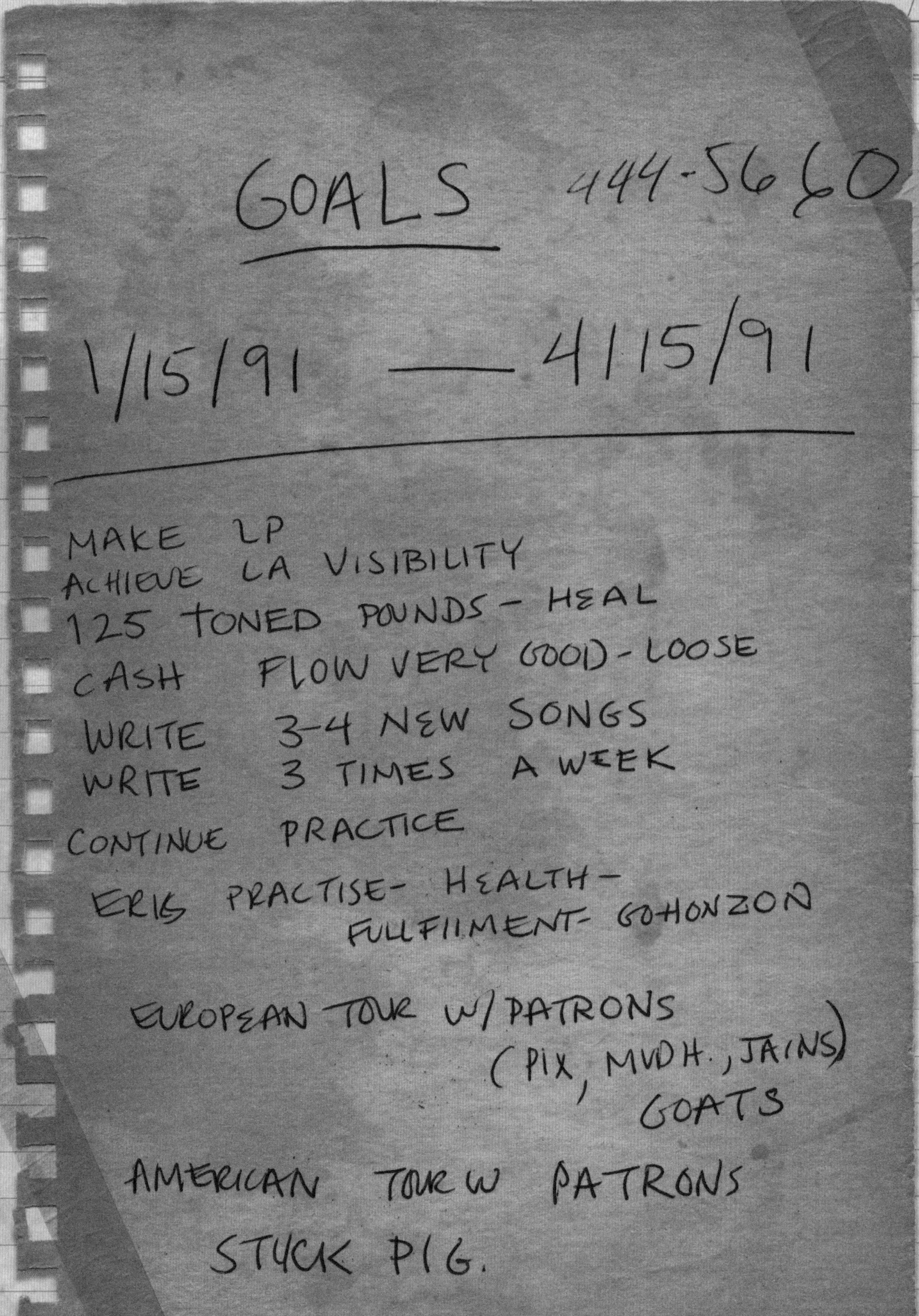

GOALS 444-5660

1/15/91 — 4/15/91

MAKE LP
ACHIEVE LA VISIBILITY
125 TONED POUNDS - HEAL
CASH FLOW VERY GOOD - LOOSE
WRITE 3-4 NEW SONGS
WRITE 3 TIMES A WEEK
CONTINUE PRACTICE
ERIS PRACTISE - HEALTH -
FULLFIIMENT - GOHONZON

EUROPEAN TOUR W/ PATRONS
(PIX, MUDH., JAINS)
GOATS

AMERICAN TOUR W PATRONS
STUCK PIG.

Jan 1, 1991

Dear miss Kim ☺

Here is a Tape of our subpop 7 wich is supposed to come out in a week or Two.

we are looking to make an LP in the next month for Sympathy ~ we had a meeting thinking of who to try for a producer and besides the fact that we would prefer working with a woman, we really like the way the STP record sounds and all admire your body of work quite hugingly & slenchingly. If you are at all interested i will give you a rehearsal tape. we would be completely honored and stoked,

Thank you Courtney Love.

Amphora vases
marjellen furniture.

Sex.

Only 2 Marriages no more.

Things That interest me: (and Everything Else Bores me.)

NAZIS
BLUES
OLD BOTTLES.
OLD BLUE BOTTLES & Tin Cans
CHRISTIANITY – CATHOLICISM
POOR BLACK/WHITE PEOPLE
BABYLONIA – (History of Iraq – Mesoptomania
mecca, Nation of Islam.)

County meath
County Cork
Provence.

Avedon
Post modern celebrity.

WB Yeats

TEAPOTS
VICTORIANA
Genealogy
Geology
Roman History
Celtic History
Astronomy
physics
molecular Biology
perverse Avant Garde literature.
poetry

Goon show
Roman History
Hamlet
monty python
Englishmen.
Irishmen.
Northern men.
Cooking well

Being a Great Fuck.
SELF GLORIFICATION
Strange sexual practises of the Famous
a certain level of my Budahist sect
Romantic intrigues
MY LIFE
ROCK
PUNK ROCK

humility.
3 children in this life
Discipline

Joy Division
Elton
Peter Sellers old Guitars
Dylan CHICK MUSICIANS.
Monroe BAD Early 80's NEW wave! ("missing persons Berliner")

Add/Scain

Hard Ball
STRATEGY
a Good spank! a Good Spankee!

True Love.

I AM AN
AMERICAN

fine delicate dainty refined,
comely. Fair Slender

thin svelte
Appealing
attractive
choice
proper
spiritual

Blue lick me
like a Drunk Bear
take the snares
out of your hair

thanks for going there.

virtuous

Hello kitty, Hello kitty, whatcha
Gonna do when the lights are peeling —

lithe When MRS. JONES
lives in my BONES
graceful AND i AM SO NUMB
Easy i AM SO Dull
handsome well bred
purified Moral Clean
intellectual
pure chaste

i pick my Dull Edge Apart
my Blunted Eye
So Easy to satisfy
NO Quotient just a Grime
that settles Every where
is it Boredly poisoning my self
I'm Not vital or real
what you think is dangerous is so stupid.

Coarse indelicate rough vulgar Corrupt
obscene Lewd impure sensual thick
dense bulky enormous monstrous fat
Corpulate large unwieldy obese
fleshy ponderous clownish rude Low
Vulgar unbecoming Repulsive total
whole

84 6
86 7
89 8
287

Go see
Yr Nazi NUN
with her
pants undone
Go Join the herd
Go Join the Herd

Lori Ann - BULLY

Oh God Not this again, sucking sucking
Not this again
There is insane & then there is Evil
shes like a mirror
held up ~~title~~ by an enemy
you just see Medusa, but Empty Empty
you just see the Vapid State of New Jersey
the stench of a Bully - in my room
she mouths the word DOG
she Hisses its Poison shes Dialing the phone
shes Dialing my phone
Redialing my phone

I have a fine burning all on my own
better than Love its mine, alone

noone can take my Flame Away
my black fucking cloud, the burning
Wont use the bad word
when you plant the bad seed
plant the bad seed
right next to me.
just like Medusa
but Empty a Bully

— MARCH 91 -

Things are going well. we are signing to Caroline and have Kim Gordon producing us, playing Beat the Clock w/ Kat, wich i choose and i am chanting regularly.
I finally sent the Great Fuck you to my Mother wich took alot of courage.
But I forgive her - I gave my word -
we are doing well, although Not as Prolific or easy to Finger as some bands and certainly not as clever-clever with Titles as pussy Galore we are still i believe heads and tails above the rest. i am frightened of the success so close and it scares me. im frightened of having it just a short time but i will overcome that i will make them
Riot i will cure them i will keep them interested i will not bend.
my Diplomatic skills are finely Tuned at last combined with a striving for purity and honesty in my lyricism
i think this LP will do well.
and be important. I Love Eric,

VOID. I want for once the phone to be picked up by my boyfriends not by their girlfriends.

WIPERS way - you've got the somewhere - silver stars I want to create there once was a

1991 - Summer.

LOVE U IN A CHEAP TRICK WAY, but NOT IN A Black Sabbath way - I'm meeting too many peoples eyes and too many of the people I'm meeting have the white hot crackle in thier eyes.

I Love you IN a T Rex Way but not → IN reclining - universe shoot out - VALUE

Hole wishes to Thank:
Kate Belljar, Long Gone John (please Stop hating us) [redacted] Subpop, Sally Borviak, Mo, Carla, Mia Ferraro, Lisa Roberts, Micheal [redacted] Geisbrecht, Errol Stewart Heather Heiged our sister Finch, RC Bottum, Joe Cole, [redacted] the Goats, Laurel, John Connors,

thanks to Everyone that was ever in this band:
Heather Errol Lisa Mike Mia Carla Rob Graves
Also Long Gone John, Jennifer Finch, Joe Cole, Subpop,
Roddy B., AL Flipside, [redacted] The Goats
[redacted] and Kate Belljar.
This record is Dedicated in Loving Memory to Rob Ritter.
I [redacted] Miss you.

I worked to hard for my Sins.
Im into my Sin and im into Vulnerability, and im into not Compromising my ideals so as to Keep my mystery or Appeal more to the Corporate mother Fuckers who would destroy this band. I mean whatever, thats my story, its so Heavy, put on some Abba or some T Rex for Fucks Sake.

this is all im going to Say to that stupid Fucking Magazine

Fuck it i wont Say Anything.

Thanks to Everyone that was ever in this Band
Rob Lisa Mike Errol Heather Mia Carla
Also Long Gone John Jennifer Finch Joe Cole Subpop, [redacted]
Roddy B. AL Flips ide the Fab Goats from NYC
Sarah and Katey Belljar - this record is Dedicated in Loving Memory to Rob Ritter
we Miss you. all the Time.

Above the boy
put me somewhere Above
the boy with all
the candy in my hand
i've seen it all before
Still cry & beg for more

I will be here watch
the sky turn violet
i want it Again
and violent more violent
more violent
and it comes to me
as no surprise
and i Looked at it
through your Twisted EYES

I wish my hands
were Turning
into skylarks
flying millions of them

Sister Hurricane
Spreadem wide
Ruby rose in
the mystic
pearl
in the wilt
you cajole
cajole to the
Eternal soulcoil Hole
saintpersephone
pray For us NOW
in the Hour of our
needs

Fuck monster Deluxe TRIPLE holy fuck
Physic stripper twisting into Ghost towns
shes Lady DISGUSTUS the FAB patroness
Holy old divine yr Everything is mine
Saint Sickly sweet of suicide and Love.

Theres noone ever to talk to
Drive, so i sit in my little
Time listening to Joan Baez.
friends in my band, me and
ones that Fight insanely.
in himself, all of his Confidence
Spine and i dont want to
i have Mojo. but i dont have
more like 20 interviews yesterday
i shutup for a second, Coz thats
Give myself away for free Free
~~stuff~~ we come off like the most
Fucks that ever walked, its
or something or maybe its the
we come off as Sincere Evil
it, I hate being in Control i
i hate how ~~these~~ these Germans Rant
Hype hype hype i hate how

in LA and i cant
shack most of the
I just wish we were
Eric are, but were the
he has no confidence
is in me. I am this
be a LEADER because
confidence... I think we did
and do you know, when
all i do .babble babble
Free, and Force them to talk
arrogant pompous Evil
that LA upbringing
Truth, at least when i talk
Fucks [illegible]. I just hate
hate not being in Control
and Rave About our
Cynical Limeys say in CONTRIVED

seen Cutesy until i saw
swiping cigs out of
"you wont look innocent"
with my sick sk'aler
are competing i
its very cool at all, least
pretty much completely Crucified
Every last member of her
A CHEERLEADER, now
are not evil, it just means
and Perky i dont hold it
(teenage popularity) but
Spirit makes it easier
boners and then spindle
Innocent and my band are
Day before i left England she
with a Bleach job just like
darkstar whore NOW ~ And i
and worked at the Autistic
are the only people i can
[redacted] here comes my
to my Compilation Tape, its
a little Leadbelly a little Blondie
Salisbury steak? I know you

with press officers
thier hands
, well thats the thing
friend, the Thing is we
hate it, i dont think
Everyone in my band was
in High school and
band was, i swear,
im sure, Cheerleaders
you were well adjusted
Against anyone ~~[illegible]~~ anymore
i think the cheerleading
for you to Give Guys
them. So her band is
Dark Star whores, and the
walked in the room
MINE. so shes Going to be a
wish i still lived in NW.
school because Autistic Kids
Really ~~[illegible]~~ Relate to.
Airplane Dinner i am listening
got Calamity Jane, Beach boys,
whatever, should i have the
asked me for Advice

They are putting my band on the
i guess thats a big deal, (its
put my Face. Neat.
Untense. Even if i do write
publishing Evenly so Everyone
ass. There is NO Hell like
1989 Hollywood, Except 1982-
like being singled out so
Friends, th[illegible] is the Thing
people for press. - im pretty Good
you HONE your SKILLS.
As Far as Ramones Free i dont
i cant Explain it and im all
Ramones. NO ramones. thats al

This Record
was our TRibute
to Leonard cohen
& Black Sabbath

Cover of the Melody Maker,
English) probably they'll just
that'll make Things Extra
it all, i split the
would at least cover their
trying to start a band in
1985 Portland, but i dont
much. Since i have no
that excite's me. Manipulating
at it because in isolation

Care, Fuck the Ramones,
alone but just.... Fuck the
i can say!

I think our next
ones probably
Going to be
our tribute to
the Beach boys
and Quantum
physics.

Seeing Germany from a hole.
Interviews, too many,
Im Lonely and sick of
talking About myself
I havent actually stopped
talking About myself
trying to teach myself the
Math of Charles & Kurt
and writing as much music
as possible all of it
unsatisfying & 2nd rate
to me.
a very beautiful tall man
interviewed me here in
Dortmund. many many
men curious, peekers
They think im a 'star'
cuz someone told them i was.
honestly i feel like a monkey.
from the zoo.

i am here
Not to make you
feel better
i am just here
to make you
feel WORSE

Last night we played a show that was so INSANE and frightening. It was just This hype thing and someone threw beer on me and slut slut slut an it was so Violent violent violent im still Shaking. Raped by a crowd. i asked for it

Oct 5

Just Got back from S.B. w/ MudHONEY ♡ MYLONNEE Last Night we played the Palace one of our Tightest sets EVER, the NE Chanted 2 hours yesterday - I was so Focused the Whole band was Focused I Focused on GRACE and the state of it i am so sick of This Pugilist Vulgarian 1 Dimensional imAGE Foisted upon me by peoples First GLANCE. i Wanted to show POISE, Melody, SPAN, Violence And we did! ~~Much~~ Much to The Corporate' Worlds DELITE apparently, at least we didnt Embarass Janet. Mark was Not Sexy. actually They sucked last Night, but Tonight ~~they~~ were Excellent Again and Mark was Sexy ~

Cant tell if im S or M. sometimes I like beating boys.

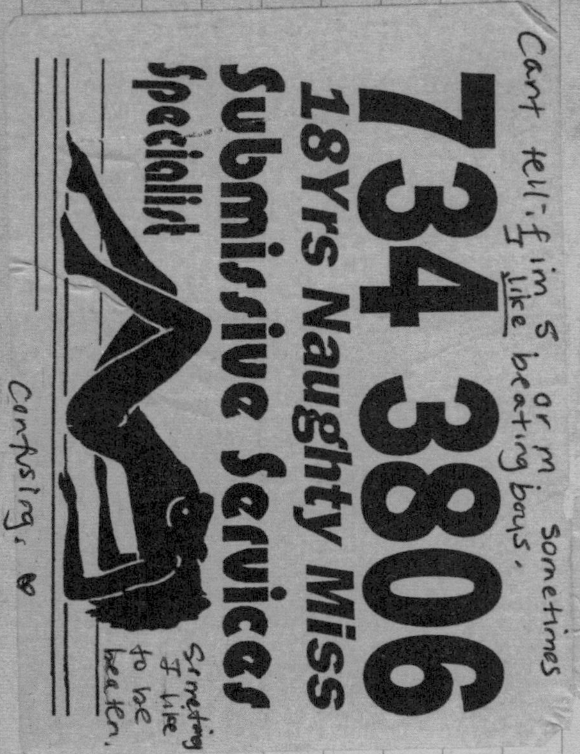

Something I like to be beaten.

Confusing. ♡

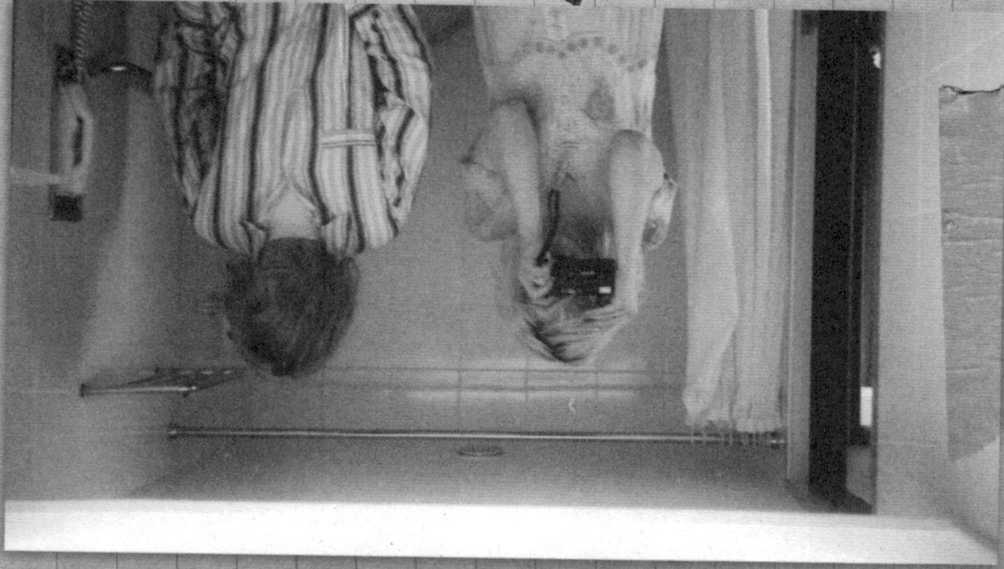

Frances Tummy ↑ in my (↑ Kurts weenie

i miss the dead brownbirds
and dirty yellow sweaters
i miss all that broken glass
that makes me feel better

There's one season here
one season all year

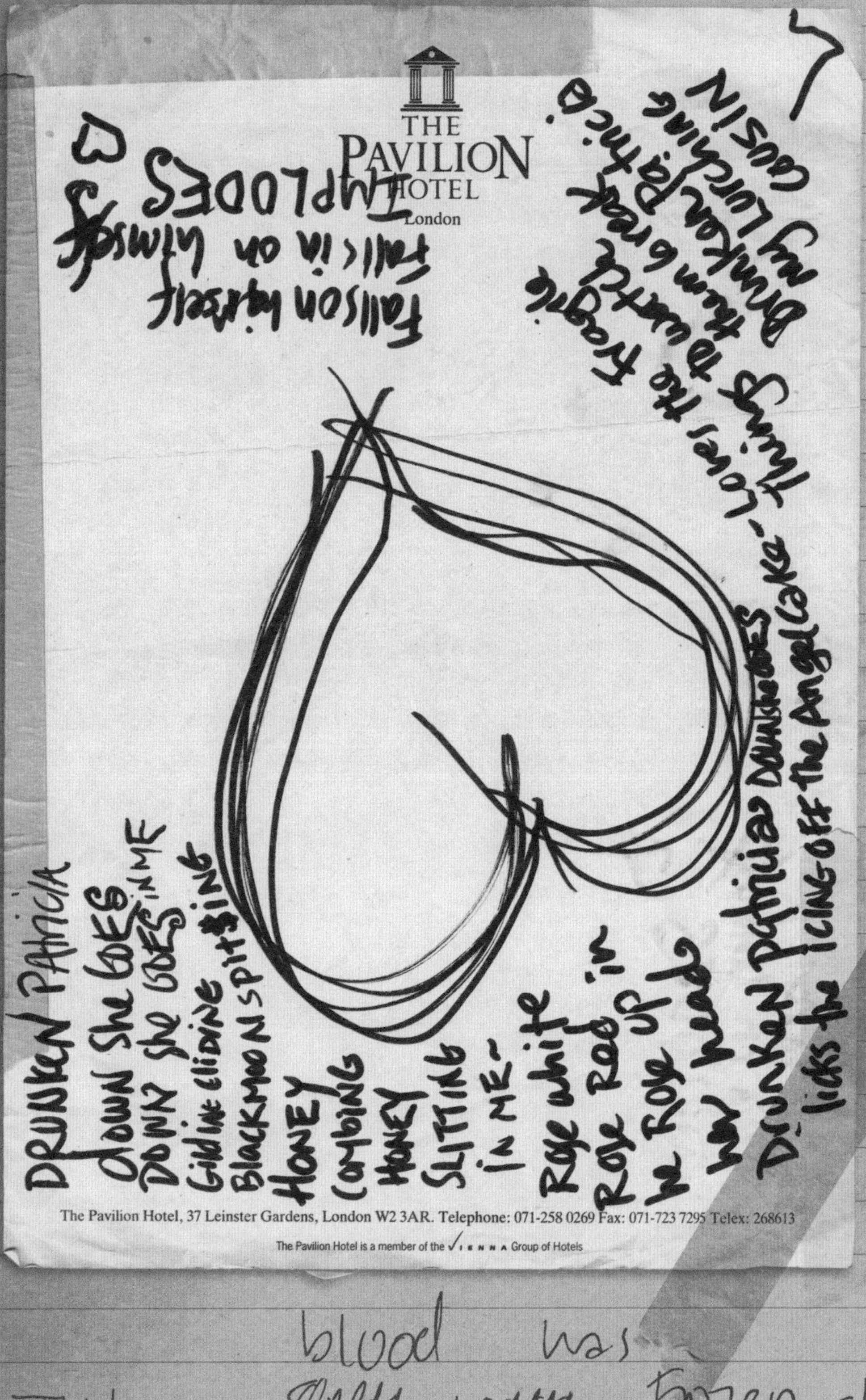

K ♡ i love him PURE
like nothing else

it feels like nothing else
its more revelatory an PURE
pixie crushing me so pretty

blood was
Til her ~~Eyes were~~ frozen slowly
and her eyes were dark & holy

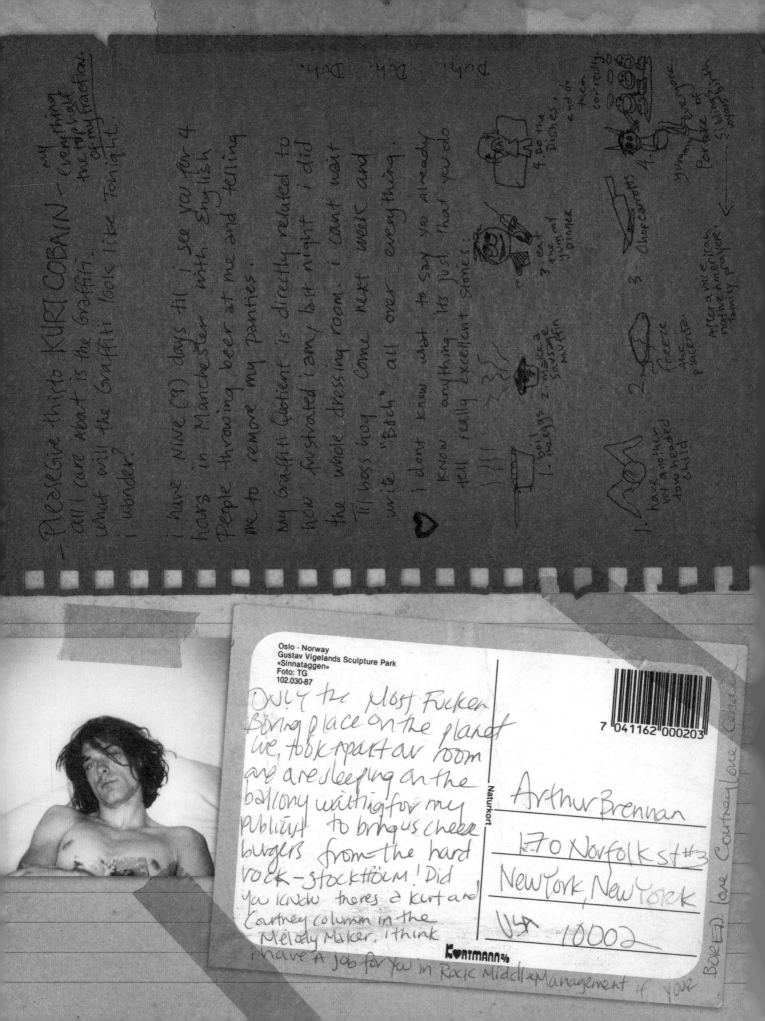

– PleaseGive this to KURT COBAIN – my everything the top half of my fraction.
all i care about is the Graffiti.
what will the Graffiti look like Tonight.
i wonder?

i have NINE (9) days til i see you for 4 hours in Manchester with English People throwing beer at me and telling me to remove my panties.
My Graffiti Quotient is directly related to how fustrated i am, but night i did the whole dressing room. i cant wait til boss hog come next week and write "Bitch" all over everything.
♥ i dont know what to say you already know anything. its just that you do tell really excellent stories:

1. boil the eggs 2. make a sausage muffin 3. eat the yummy Dinner 4. Do the Dishes, and do them correctly.

1. have yet another tow headed child 2. freeze the placenta 3. Chop carrots 4. yummy everyone Partake of 5! blings birth onions

After a nice native american family prayer. ←

Duh. Duh. Duh.

Oslo - Norway
Gustav Vigelands Sculpture Park
«Sinnataggen»
Foto: TG
102.030-87

ONLY the Most Fucken Boring place on the planet we took apart our room and are sleeping on the balcony waiting for my publicist to bring us cheese burgers from the hard rock – stockholm! Did you know theres a kurt and Courtney column in the Melody Maker. i think i have a job for you in Rock Middle Management if your BORED. love Courtney love Cobain

Naturkort

Arthur Brennan
170 Norfolk st #3
New York, New York
USA 10002

7 041162 000203

KORTMANN A/S

i once had to have the boy down the street be my Babysitter and he was a year younger, i wish it would have been you i Guarantee you'd have been TWICE as fucked up. i used to torture him without Mercy. i used to tell him i was Going to introduce him to my Friend SATAN. i told him SATAN visited me every NIGHT and FUCKED me. he Quit, he got so scared of me: I told him my Lion came alive at night and went into the dreams of my enemies and made them into retards and he believed me.

in the tape. luv. Courtney

Oslo - Norway
Gustav Vigelands Sculpture Park
«Sinnataggen»
Foto: TG
102.030-87

Kurt played with Extreme and Pearl Jam the other day. It was FuckenA hot. Imagine a sea of 40,000 perfect blond people that don't know the difference between Nuno Bettencourt & Nirvana. The Baby's kicking all the time

Now Back next week — Come pick it up

Naturkort

Long Gone John
4901 Virginia Ave
Long Beach, CA
USA 90805

7 041162 000203

KORTMANN a/s

Hi AL and Foes I played a guitar solo for Nuno Betencourt the Guitar player for extreme Pearl Jam Broke up. oh the Guilt! the Guilt! love Kurdt

Oslo - Norway
Gustav Vigelands Sculpture Park
«Sinnataggen»
Foto: TG
102.030-87

God were really big in europe I PROMISE.... i wish Carlos would stop thinking that my band selling 10 records is like... A MIRACLE... because now i look really dumb. oh well what Else is New. I'm on The ROAD WITH MY OLD MAN and its pretty sick, but he did play with PEARL JAM AND EXTREME the other DAY. Fuckin Ⓐ Hot BABY, i Got stripsearched Today coz im 7 months pregnant and they thought the baby was

Hot... LOVE COURTNEY LOVE

Naturkort

AL FLIPSIDE.

7 041162 000203

KORTMANN a/s

but i love you. Dont worry About it.

AND

SHES NOT EVEN

Annoying people, by and large, are treated like dirt. Doors slam in our faces. The kids at school scorn us! Mock us! Kick us! Ignore us! Call us names! Irritators, people like me, need a voice, however out of tune it may be! We deserve equal treatment! All except the ones who scratch their fingernails against chalkboards.

Sarah Hammond, 14, Oberlin, OH

PRETTY

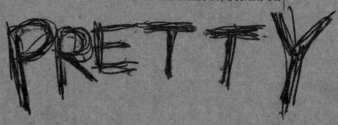

VOL I
SPRING 92

thats why Boys should carry our AMPS!

"There are some jobs women do as well as men. But we still aren't equal, mentally or physically."
Nicky Davis, 20, from Tunbridge Wells.

"Job-wise, women should have equality, but this is ideological. A woman's place is in the home, and always will be."
Rosslyn Ebbetts, 18, from Harrow.

I WANT A WHORE FROM HELL That Loves the PIXIES and the GERMS. WHERE ARE YOU???

Now that Ive been through Female Castration from marrying a ROCKSTAR, i want a Bass player in my band A REVOLUTIONARY, Inspired by those Hot D.C. Bitches, someone who can play ok, and stand in Front of 30,000 people, take off Her shirt and have FUCK YOU written on Her TITS, If your Not Afraid of me, and your Not Afraid to FUCKING SAY IT, SEND A LETTER: PO BOX 3111, LA CA, 90078, HOLE 213-969-9173

NO MORE PUSSIES, NO MORE FAKE GIRLS

HATE

1 Nirvanamania
2 OLYMPIA
3 GIRLS that call my house NO matter how cool
4 EX-GIRLFRIENDS of husband (NO matter How cool)
5 BEING PREGNANT
6 MAJOR LABEL BIDDING WAR
7 Minneapolis
8 Pearl Jam, Nymphs, etc. shit,
9
10 DRUGS
11 SASSY
12 Everett

LOVE

1 DRUGS
2 YOKO ONO
3 Kim and Thurston
4 Husker Dü
5 Helping Bands.
6 Calamity Jane
7 The Bikini Kill
8 N.O.Ulysses 7 inch
9 GUS VAN ZANT
10 NIRVANAMANIA

11. Sassy
12. Everett

She Didnt have a best friend. No shit.

DID she?

well?

Answer me! Answer me!

Is it better to out-monster the monster or to be quietly devoured? — Friedrich Nietzsche

EX - BEST FRIENDS (Male, Dead, cont)

LOVED PUNK ROCK

*** Pisces, Junkie Faggot, Taught me Every Chord i Know on Guitar, Drummed in my band for 10 minutes, knew every punk rock song and made out with Darby, was in the Bags, the Nymphs, and 45 Grave, (all female led).,
Had Rad Sex one Stoned NIGHT, Lived off my strip money for months (I was Glad to share) I used to stare up at the violet lights when i lay on the Floor During "THIRD SONG" (thats the pussy shaver song) and think about his Elizabeth Taylor eyes. How the Fuck Do you think He died?

I love you Soecide.

*** ARIES
SHOT IN THE MOTHERFUCKING HEAD BY SOME SATANIC LANDSHARK (Yeah, im sorry he was black, Okay?)
WHEN COMING HOME FROM MY SHOW WITH HENRY ROLLINS — STUCK UP FOR ME ALWAYS - BRAVE AND STRONG AND UNDERSTOOD WOMEN MORE THAN ANYONE, ROADIED FOR US OUR LAST TOUR - WE WATCHED A GUY DIE IN BALTIMORE (SHOT IN THE HEAD AT OUR FEET) MADE OUT AT 4AM, JUST TO PROVE WE WERE ALIVE

LOVED PUNK ROCK

the fake smile on the nurses face drip drip drip

tear the petals off of you and make
you tell the truth
tie it iff gag it
make him feel better(cant you make him feel better
your coming hearts an d stars
on your little yellow sweater
ritalin doll
queen of the mall
fairy pink sugar
SHE BLOWS THE DEATH RATTLE
ICE CREAM ON MY DRESS
HES COLD GET HIM A CANDYCOAT
ICE CREAM ON MY BIB

Reposition the clitoris
Sewup the Vagina for a Snugger fit
Loosen the throat Muscles
Sever the Gag Reflex
Chronic sedated slimness

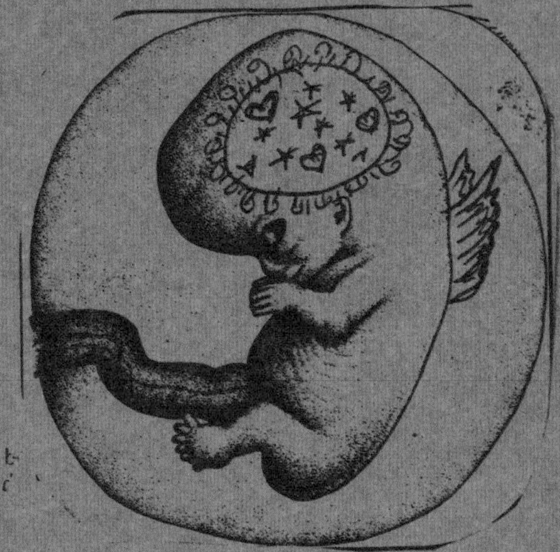

Many artists and exex, while acknowledging that pressures to show a little leg are still strong in some quarters, say such tactics wouldn't work for the new female bands.

BUT I GUESS IT DOESNT FUCKING HURT

INSTRUCTIONS FOR FACIAL SURGERY

COURTNEY LOVE

The purpose of cosmetic surgery is to make you look as good as it is possible for you to look. It cannot do more than that. If you are expecting a transforming miracle from surgery, you will unquestionably be disappointed. It is impossible to guarantee results. The ultimate goal of cosmetic surgery is to achieve a natural improved appearance.

You should bear in mind that with some patients undergoing facial surgery, there is a temporary period of slight emotional depression immediately following the surgery during the period when you look your worst. This is quite normal and should not alarm you. It is not easy to look bruised and swollen, particularly when natural expectations are toward improvement of your appearance. Fortunately this period passes quickly.

APPROXIMATELY THREE WEEKS BEFORE YOU WILL BE ABLE TO SING

raining
tear the doll to pieces throw the head awa
i only love the fragile things
cos i love to see them break
all waste4 and void
all waste and void
all wastye and void

down where the whores lie down,leave me

crawling up the wall on the back of a vicious red insect,craling

feverishly toward the gaping rim of some kicked in wall hole. the pl
ace where the X meets the exit (from my slavery).

22222222222

bleeding from one of my innumerable cutterages,come here
little girl i want you to reluieve me,i wish i had a cock to stuff
in your big dollbaby stupid ass face
but ill have to be satisfied beating you into a
breathless breathing heavy jellypulp and throwing
your lazy ass out into the piss corridor.
find a voice? i am sure. i found one. the swish
of that pigs blood as it pummeled onto Carries head.
worship now
worship now
worship now what i am about to destroy.
i slash me.
i knife mine.
i slash me
i knife mind.
acid stars, long jagged scars,
the cut worm forgives the plow
in the twisted roots of an oak he was suspended
in a fungus wich hung on a hook head downwards
into the deep breeding reptiles in his mind.
a vast spine writhing. the prolific and the devouring worms in
side, gelid and frosty. the dancing dogs and bears
the wretched blind pit ponies,the
little hunted hares.
the bad eyes watching us in the bloody mud. the one thats cocked
sunsister,
sister ecto plasme shes incredulous
in her snow white pumps she takes off her dress
smash me open like a pro
silver eyes veining
he cuts me up raining
i will follow you down the sick drain
when i lean on the sink
and the angeldust gets in my eyes,my hair,
on acid stars, im getting there
lured by soda pop murders
kether,ether suck me under
ill be your three legged donkey sister
your piss Christ
thread ,my bones through your clean needle

Donna, this girl in my class, picks on everyone for no reason. She acts like she's better than everyone and thinks she's really popular—but she's not. Everyone's afraid to tell her off because she's so tough: She's sort of a gangster. But I think she needs to be told to leave people alone. Should I tell her?

will sell before its time.
MELVINS
COWS
HOLE
You cant Rape the WILLING!
DEATH LEMON ACT
show starts 9:00
MAY 23rd LINGERIE THURSDAY

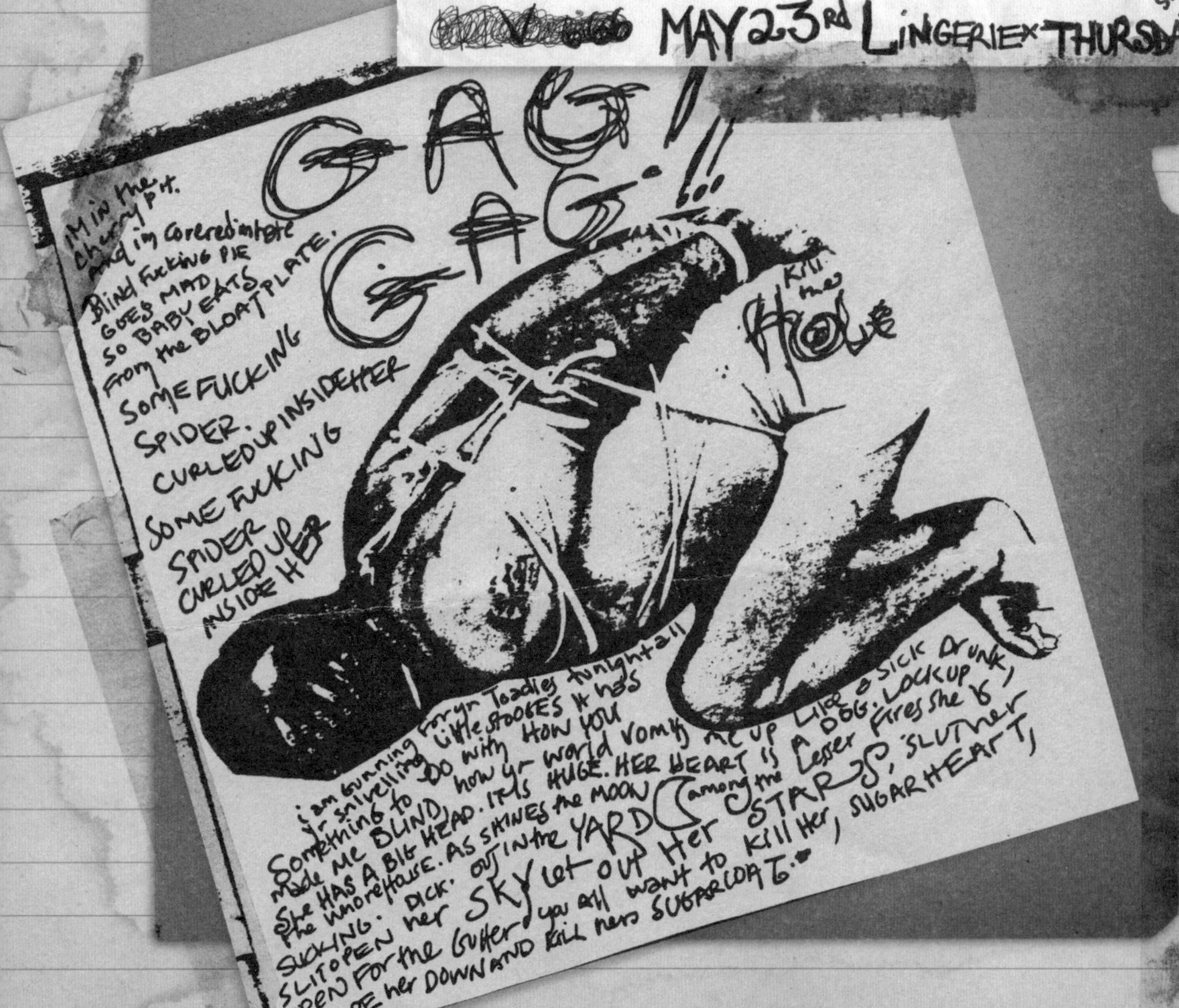
GAG! GAG! GAG!
IM in the cherry pit.
Blind Fucking pie goes mad so baby eats from the bloatplate.
SOME FUCKING SPIDER. CURLED UP INSIDE HER
SOME FUCKING SPIDER CURLED UP INSIDE HER
Kill me
HOLE
i am running for yr Toadies tonight all yr snivelling little stooges it has something to do with how you made me blind, how yr world vomits me up like a sick drunk,
She HAS A BIG HEAD. IT'S HUGE. HER HEART is A DOG. LOCK UP the whorehouse. AS SHINES the MOON among the Lesser stars she is SUCKING DICK. out in the YARD
SLIT OPEN her SKY let out Her STARS, SLUT her OPEN for the Gutter you all want to kill Her, SUGARHEART, RAPE her DOWN AND Kill hers SUGARCOAT.

FAX to Kitty Cobain ROOM#15

what would the ROSE do?
would the rose hire a publicist?

lets be mountain junkies and breed
satanic mall rats.

I am Doll parts bad skin Doll heart
it stands for knife for the rest of my Life.

peel my little heart off and soak
it in your
left hand
and call
me
Tonight

pearl jam is opening at CBS
for us. ha. ha.

[redacted]

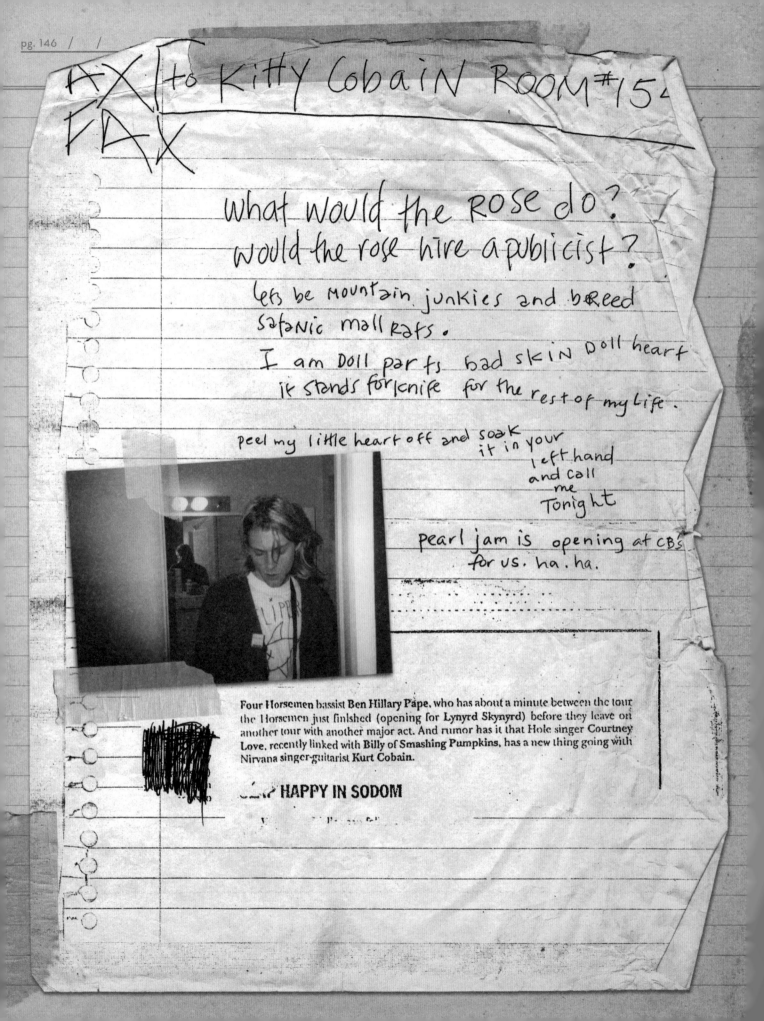

Four Horsemen bassist **Ben Hillary Pape**, who has about a minute between the tour the Horsemen just finished (opening for **Lynyrd Skynyrd**) before they leave on another tour with another major act. And rumor has it that Hole singer **Courtney Love**, recently linked with **Billy of Smashing Pumpkins**, has a new thing going with Nirvana singer-guitarist **Kurt Cobain**.

HAPPY IN SODOM

Operation cutie people.

There are 10-20,000 Cutie People on Planet Earth – i want them all to love me.

011392-4

Seeking
Sadomasochistic annihilation
of seperatate identities.
Collapsing into me.
Noone is as big. we are biggest.

FUCK ROCK
Kill ROCK
Fuck Rock
Love Rock love Rock
Kill ROCK

The PeeGirl has a Dick
your milk makes me sick
the PeeGirl Gets the Belt
your milk makes me melt

mumbling little secrets
theres creatures in the corner
all winter long
were Going to be warm
i cant name my top 10 Albums

Belt

pg. 1

It needs to die. It'd be much cooler to
have Poets and writers.
ok ok, i want to kill it.
I can see right through it. like Camille
Paglias Theory of Baudelaire, Secretly massively
desiring to be a submissive lesbian.
I can see it smell it and it, makes me,
Happy.

Things I want.
Brilliant & Best & Most Honest songs.
STRONG PRACTICE
Kurts happiness.
Erics happiness
English press
Video.
English shows
Tour Managers
Solid relationship. True Love.
Baby.
Integrity
Sincerity
Compassion
Respect
Appetite - Photos - skin.
KIDS

Shakabuku
own Gohonzon

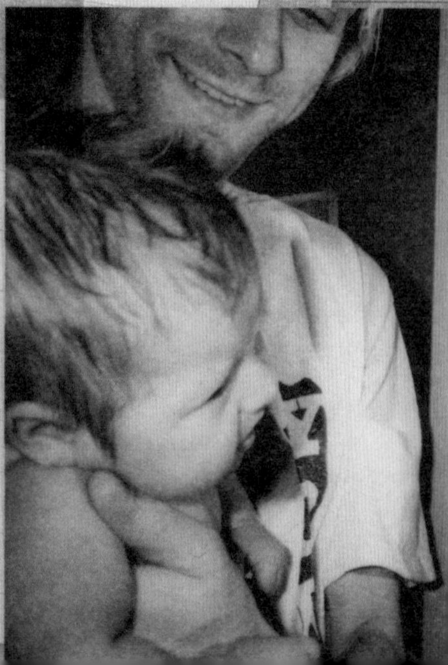

Baby's First word: pee.

Its so pure This
filthy mess
when he spills ice cream down my dress
K is for knife For the rest of my LifE

(C) (K) ? i dont care. i dont care
i dont Fucking I dont
Fucking care, I dont care,
I just dont, Fucking,
care. you can have my
cake, and my ice cream
just dont take me
from [illegible]. mE

At least i have a brain

and a voice and bleached blonde
haire.

DC DC DC DC
- Give me you - at home -

let me, Go, home,

i want to go home.

Kittys alive
shes in the bath
i cant read to good but i can do math

i am the Girl - you know
who drowns inside my bath
i can read real good
but i cant do math.

inside her head planes crash.
the truth is all rotten
it ruins yr teeth like candy cotton
my sweet tooth has burned a hole
my sweet tooth burned a hole
in your head
NOW look youve spoiled her rotten
it ruins yr teeth like candy cotton
Go to sleep under a rock
teething in my heart shape box
Theres the sad result

i hope the sperms all were deformed
i hate this box i hate it here
Im spoiled and only half formed
i hate it here - i hate it here
the sperms swimming on my legs
What a waste,
What a waste of milk and Eggs

the only Quote I've ever seen
You say about sexism its always stuck
with me. you said "I've been thrown
down the stairs more times than
i can count" this is the
moment Chrissie, i wanna
know? Did you read
backlash?

you changed my life
more than Runaways, more
than Patti, because you
wrote it, and lyrically

you are a goddess,
you are classic,

OK Closing
Chrissie.
I love you.

DAVID GEFFEN

August 18, 1992

Ms. Courtney Love
Mr. Kurt Cobain
c/o Cedars-Sinai
Room 3108
8700 Beverly Blvd.
Beverly Hills, CA 90048

Dear Courtney and Kurt,

Congratulations on your new baby girl. This is a very exciting time - you must be thrilled. I'm sure that she will bring you much laughter and happiness.

Kurt, I know that you are upset about the recent article on Courtney and the attacks made on her character. I sympathize with what you're going through and how it can affect you. The press have a way of sabotaging your privacy. The thing you have to remember is that these things pass and people quickly forget about articles of this type. You just have to let your life go on.

Please know that I am here if you need me. This should be a time of joy and celebration and I realize it's been difficult. I'll help you get through it in any way that I can.

Warmest regards,

David

David Geffen

DG:sb

KURT
COBAIN

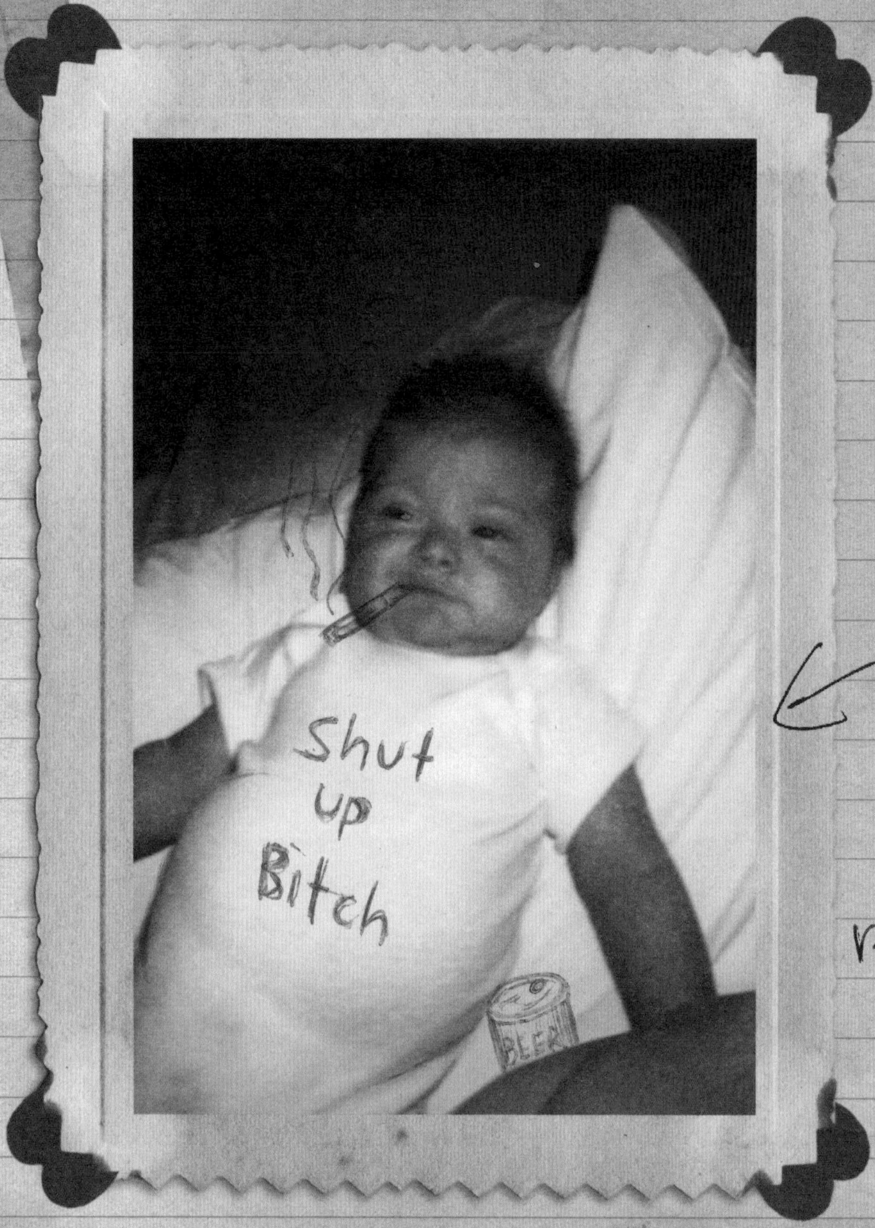

Kurt wrote that not me. based on AXL Rose telling me to shut up

Live Through This

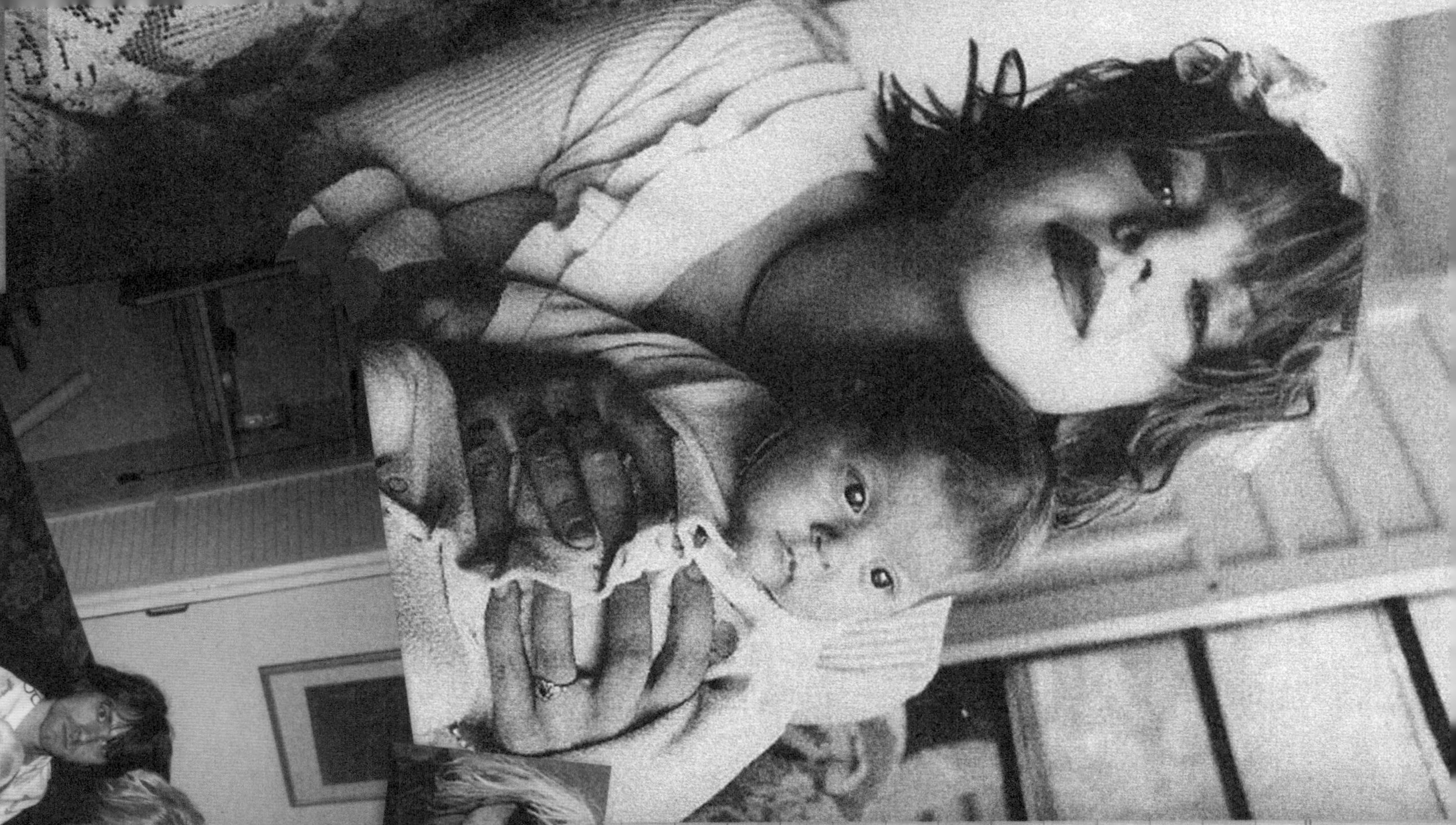

NOV 93 – Baby Gym —

She is so utterly perfect.
so full of sweet purity.
She is so utterly loving lovely
and thank God we can afford
Core for her. my First entry ever
Abrut E. Bean. – because there are no
words in English to describe the
Beauty my Daughter brings to me
Doe eyes Gazelle features

 Eclipse

Teratagonic

He takes my time away
i wasnt doing nothing Anyway

I always knew he had it in him
Stuck in some artery or tendon
put him on liquids
and take at his larnyx
and hell be happy.
hell be happy.

butter-melt
stutter-welt
boil-smelt
spoil-felt
toil-felt

* Do you wanna be a Rock star
i think you wanna be a Rock star
you say youd rather die
i think youd like to try
howd you like to be Madonna
oh i know you wanna
howd you like to be Nirvana
youd rather die!
i know you wanna, wanna be a rockstar,
rather die than be a rockstar, oh yeah.

Eyes like Angel wings
& scary kisses killing me
w/ his Eyes wide open
w/ his Eyes wide open
he could see Every-thing

Shut up. i see you.
your too close. Everything in you
i want to touch too much.

Nothing More Pure than yr disease
and the Rings on the Sun when U give it to me
and the Rips and the tears
when you Stare into me

olympia?

i lived in a Rockstars
house once.

Hitlers Girlfriend black forest Cake
Spit curls let them eat shit
* rose white / rose red rose upon my head
rose white / rose red i wanna die in this bed
hes fond of her curves
incredible bra of Eva braun
the Geli Roll shot thru' the head
Hooks and Garters
Guarantee, youll get inside of me.
and God i know youll never leave

rose white rose red
i look great when
your dead
i love my smother
yours is gone

noone Recorded this show!

English Girl
im Gonna let you Go
Your not a slag.
your not a slut.
your not a witch.
been through too much.
Liverpool Girl Gets called a slut.
Fat cow.
by idiots by bozos by creeps.
English Girl
reinvent yourself, for keeps
Your the prettiest Girl. i have ever seen. you are fucking breath-taking
Your cold in winter
and tea allday
and bedsit Girl throw down the Jackie & the NME. Fuck that shit.
English Girls are better Come home with me.
than any Girls.
they have it harder
than any Girls i know.
They dont have much money
Theyre always Cold
English Girl
im Gonna let you Go Come & Go with me
and Come and Live with me.
Im Gonna buy you sweaters and
make you drink Coffee
and Swear real loud and punch out boys
and steal cars and shoot off Guns
oh English Girl, i swear well have FUN.
Come home with me. Come and Go with me.

you left me lying
in spasm & descent
choking on yr Candy Flesh
Bury me in 1000 degrees
& SUGAR runs from yr Arteries

EVEN THE UGLIEST AMONG US

have you ever felt
like a monster.
have you ever felt
so ASHAMED. felt
have you ever felt. so ugly.
so ugly. so ugly.
SO UGLY. as me.

i want to know
HOW BIG IS YR SOUL

is it BIG As the MOON
is it Dead as the MOON

HAVE

Shes sweet baby
want to rape her head
want to cross her eyes
want to rape her dead.
Shes sweet baby
mystic Tornado
shes so cold
Needs a SUGARCOAT

Cradle my Girdle
it holds me in
my Adipose sin

Didnt i beg youpray

I found you in my milky tea
it took my hole for you to me.

help me im purity
hit me im shivering
he wants to see stars shrivel on icy Angel Ache

(and) the Virgin milk, i chole from Holywater
(and the hymen of the Queen)
Lily Lily mystic rose
Honeysuckle, God - damn mystic rose
thread my bones through your clean needle
Use once and destroy

my blisters defy desire
the husk of him.
you got the body.
i keep the Fire.

BEAUTY SLASHING
WIERD LAUGHING

you left me lying in Spasm and descent
gagging on your virgin flesh
have you ever felt so Ashamed?
" as ugly.
as ugly.
as ugly as me.

WORSHIP NOW
WORSHIP NOW
What I am About to Destroy

How big is yr soul. is it dead like the moon.
is it black like my hole.

Tear that Doll to Pieces
Throw its head Away
Mother Vulture Shes insane

MADE OUR

the sugar star
the Mother whore
watch me Dissapear
i got the Bulysed hand
Every Time your near me

Sit in the Cornerand Drink Drown Soda
bomb the whole State of minnesota
Have U Ever felt... As ugly as me.
Im on my bad knee
that Porno made a Lady out of me

I one eye Gulp
the Honey blood
the Honey blood
of my Sugarheart

LOVERS

Icing on the
cake now my
bandaid is undead

BEG

the swish of blood
on Carries head
Im eating you
an' overfed

unreal chemical peel
lips are fake.

Drives a Nazi car

The oldest

As a chronic runaway pothead in Skipworth Juvenile home, the next logical step for me was to commit some tedious felony and end up using wasted space in a jail as an adult. I thank GOD for the young intern Steve who just returned from ~~...~~ the back vacation in the UK; he gave me 3 records to play in the "Library", a room full of "books" — Every Harlequin romance' Every written and a handful of Readers Digest condensed Novels — Sitting amor

well i went to skool
in Olympia
and Everyones the same
well what do yer do with a revolution
Yeah you forget your name
well i went to skool in a Fascist state
and everyones the same we got it great
maximum ~~we~~ got punk rock ~~and were better than you~~ &
yeah yeah yeah
Wont you please make me real, Fuck you
sick
punk Fuck you!

well i went to school
in olympia - & Everyones the same
from Parasites to psychopaths
please please please leave me alone
and i went to school at punk rock high
and Everyones the same
weve got a little REVOLUTION
and Everyone knows our name
well i went
(the Fascists & the nerds went away

Ophelia, our hero, NOT

Linernotes Live thru this Marietta GA. 1993

Hellokitty. I am trash from Planet Dogstar.
Kling on Eyefire. like a virus on Glucose. your hungry. but. Im. STARVING.
i used to Live in Hollywood. i saw Miss Mercy
on the bus. it was Morning after a Trashy Night.
She was Going to Meet Arthur lee in a parking Lot.
Dont sell your publishing. keep the Negatives.
and take the Cadallac its all your Going to Get.
i have a Germs burn. Noone in portland
ever believed my LA stories and i burned with
the desert Expanse. a leper thumbelina
with a stupid desire to Challenge... certain....
phallocentric institutions. Well, J. i hope my Lillypad
Grows directly on your Smooth pond like a stubborn weed.
and i hope i languidly recline in that awful smog heat and
psychotic state of "celebrity". my hero/ines are
Hamlet, Prince of Denmark, Echo and the Bunnymen, Robert Zimmerman,
Darby Crash, Bette Davis and maybe Perry Farrell.
This is a Dairy Album because the privelage of Suckling
was removed from my arms and because Motherhood is
like • Wolf. and the Milk stayed in me and became
bileous and CUNTLIKE. Smooth and Flappy. Rosebud pink
and Also Flappy and Liver spotted. Cunt LIKE... i was moved
to purchase Arms and Ammo. i wish i was beautiful or at least
wise but im simply mad and violent. still, as an American
i have my rights. And noone wants Lenny Bruce at the End
of his Career. ive got some stolen Karl Lagerfield shoes from
a shoot. ha. ha. And i am Sullen Demure Maternity
Dignity and Grace kelly and oh what a Liar.

i dream of Anne Sexton in her Red Negligee with her therapist.
i dream of Four years in Hillcrest state school.
i dream of LIFE, WIFE, and Truth. Now.

GO TO HELL.

Courtney.

SUNSET MARQUIS

Hotel and Villas

Kurt and Frances
Bean

I love you
please forgive me.
please Frances
you are
both too beautiful
for me ♡
I love you 4ever

1200 North Alta Loma Road, West Holl
Tele

April 17th

from Mrs C.L. Cobain:

S

Times:

Nothing will ever again be the same.
~~from April 1st onward,~~
Exactly one month ago today
was the last time i made Love
with my husband. i cooked him
Dinner. We spent 4 hours in the playroom
with Frances, we saw "schindlers list"
it made us frightened ~~of~~ OR life and
we spoke of the value of life. our
convictions, we defined, until 4 am
and we fell asleep in each others arms
and woke up that way in the morning.
Rome was a huge cover up, and i see it
now.... i just didnt want to see it then.
last night i reread the note he left
-in Rome- its so obviously a
suicide note, So fucking obvious.
After 22 hours of prayer and chanting
he came down from the Ceiling

grow

new heart

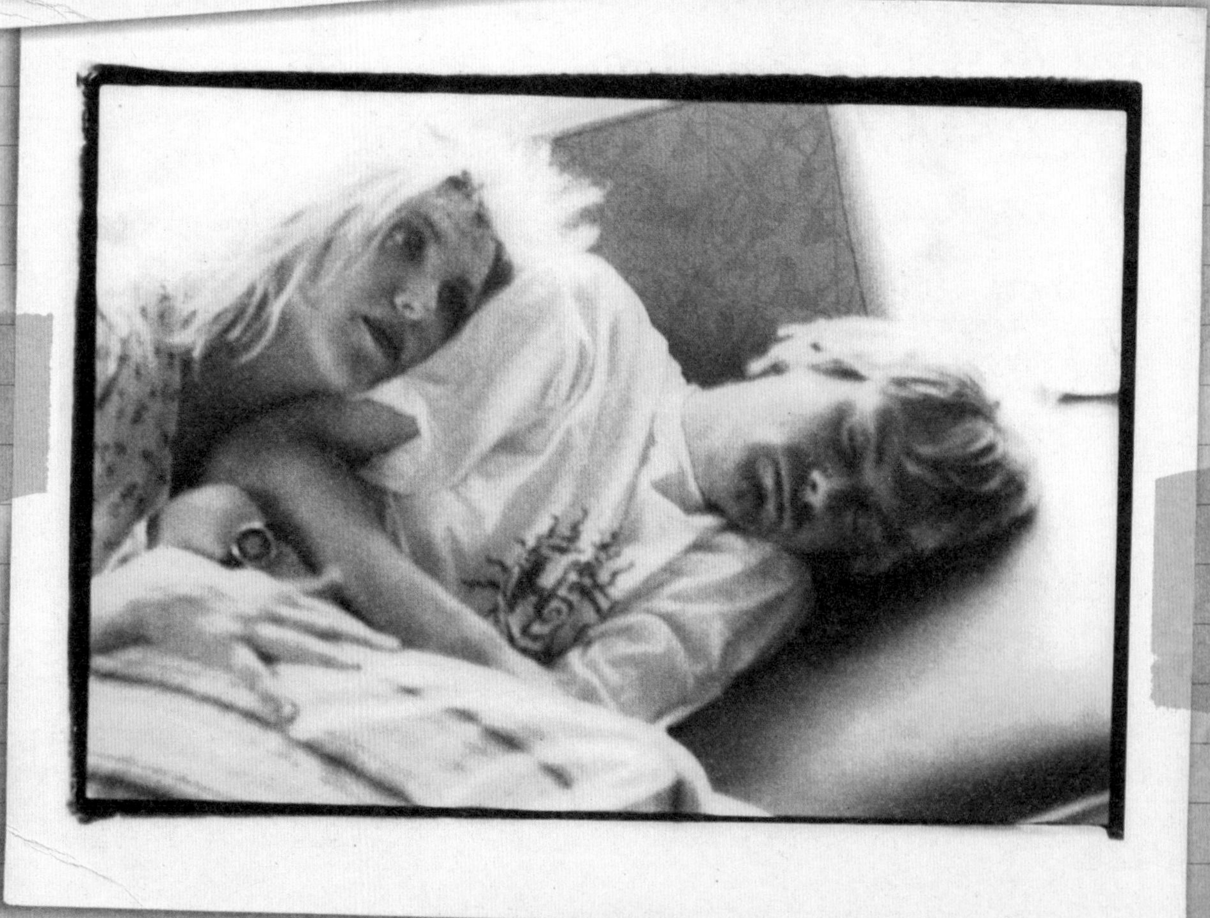

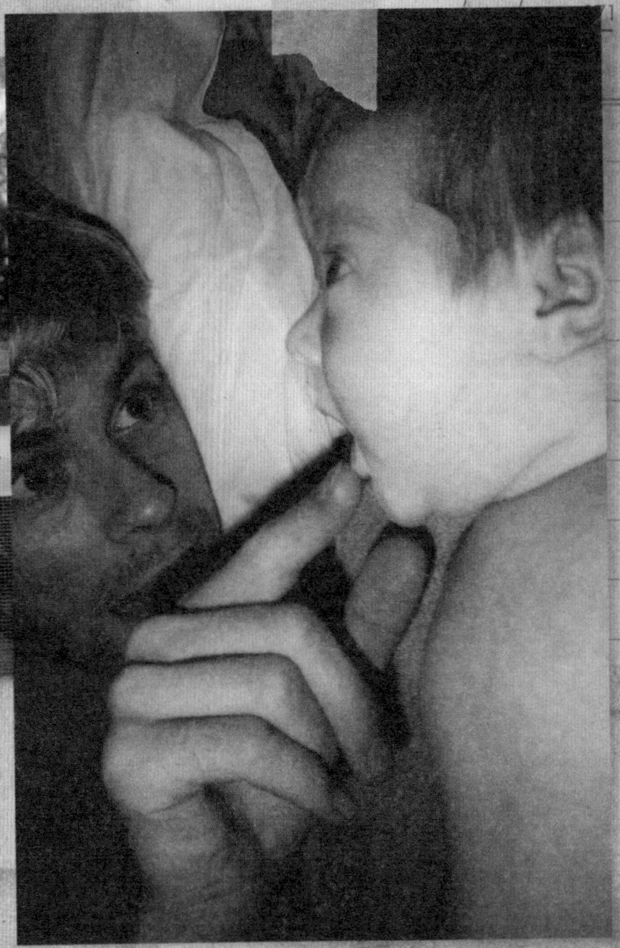

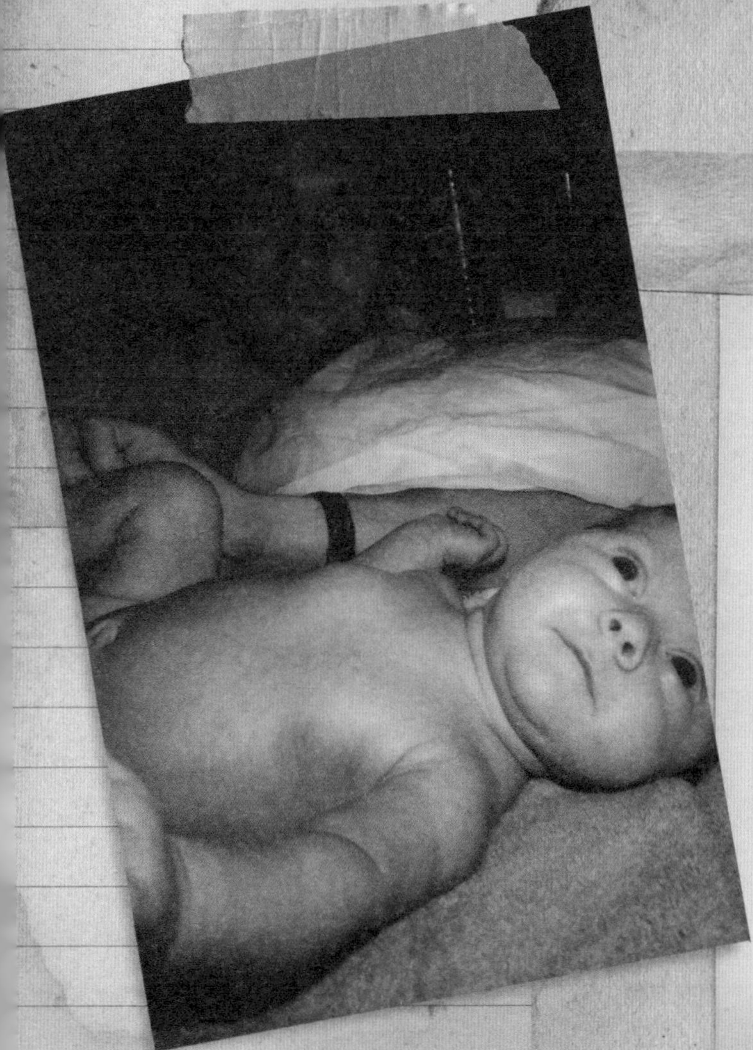

- DaDUY and mister meows

Cobain Mort i left the boy lifeless
Streetcar named Succubus
~~beneath her~~
the stars
beneath her
the sky
and enter into
the forest in the darkest part
my ancestor was the core of discovery
you never hear of him
Shiva
was he the Drunk in the bunch?
was he the illiterate one?
I come from the stock of the staff
they say i drained your gold
they say i left your silver

dear boy
dear box of chocolates
Tamper not your pretty bones
and sewn shut eyes
Fear not. the plague has passed
the stone has no Tomb. .
sweet baby.

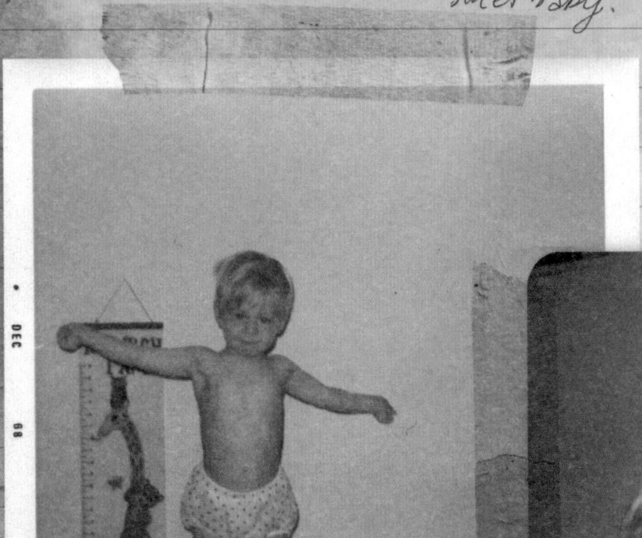

Today my Gardener and i transplanted a weeping willow. the people from the Japanese garden Come by and oohed-aaahed over the present garden little banzai trees and tiny Japanese Maple. i hate it, its too proscieunt. i mean POINTY and POSTMODERN these woomen got even more disgusted when they heard of my plans to plant a jungle of Lilacs and tear down the Horrible shrubs

Roses are horrible snobs they will only grow in soil that is only growing OTHER ROSES, they cant stand the company of anything but there own speciium. and the tiny Japanese are even snoolier than the Roses. it has to be the same exact type of plant.
-and roses are strange the insanely beautiful hybrids dont breed at all and the gorgeous sexy hybrids dont smell or reproduce

but the ones that smell the best (grasse - rose Absolut, mideastern - damask roses) are butt. ugly one whole section of the property is a trellis and a tree trunk and its going to be completely bone / blue white from march til August its going to be - exploding white, foaming right outside the bedroom window, from the Dogwood and Magnolia and Apple blossoms down to the teeniest Muguet lily of the valley and Lowest Casablance Lilies, its going to be:
INSANE, the jewel of the County
I planted this weeping willow today and we (Canegan — Dylan and i) put his ashes in the roots

→

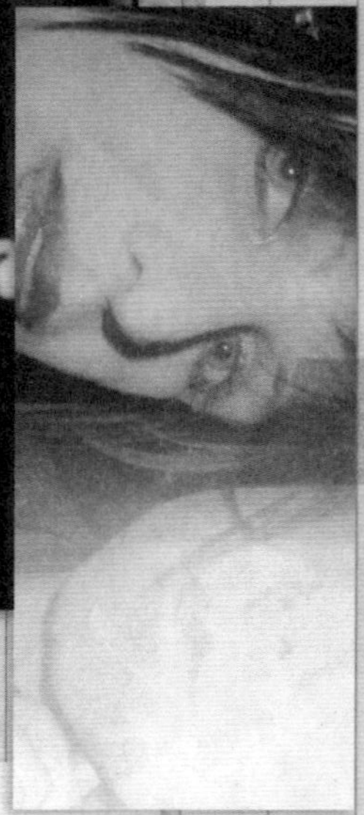

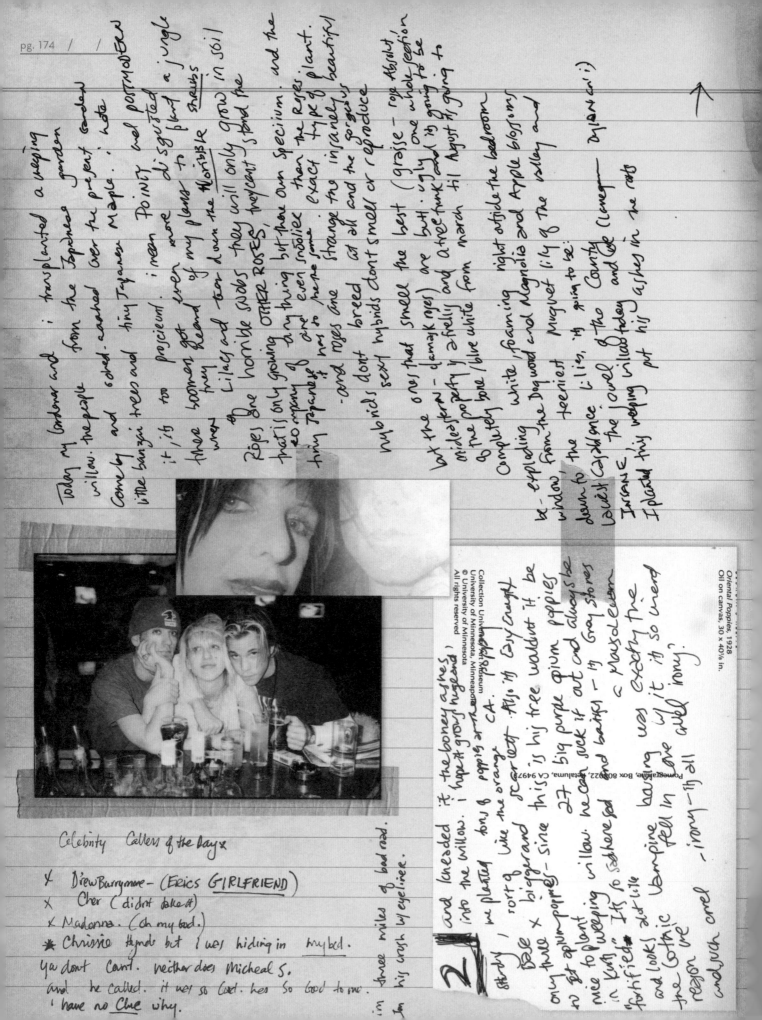

Celebrity Callers of the Day ×

× DrewBarrymore - (Erics GIRLFRIEND)
× Cher (didnt take it)
× Madonna. (oh my God.)
✱ Chrissie Hynde but I was hiding in my bed.
ya dont Care. neither does Micheal S.
And he called. it was so Cool. hes So Good to me.
i have no Clue why.

im three miles of bad road.
Im his crush w/ eyeliner.

2 and kneaded it the boney ashes, into the willow. i hope it grows huge and sturdy, we planted tons of poppies at the CA. poppy Base sort of like the orange scarlett Also its Easy Enough only three × bigger and since this is his tree wouldnt it be nice to plant 27 big purple opium poppies to get opium poppies - in Kurts weeping willow. he can suck it out and always be "fortified" Its so sad here sad and beautiful - its Gray stones and looks alot like a Mausoleum the Gothic Vampire having was exactly the reason we fell in love w/ it its so wierd and such cruel - irony - its all cruel irony?

Oriental Poppies, 1928
Oil on canvas, 30 x 40⅛ in.
Collection University Art Museum
University of Minnesota, Minneapolis
© University of Minnesota

Pomegranate, Box 808022, Petaluma, CA 94975

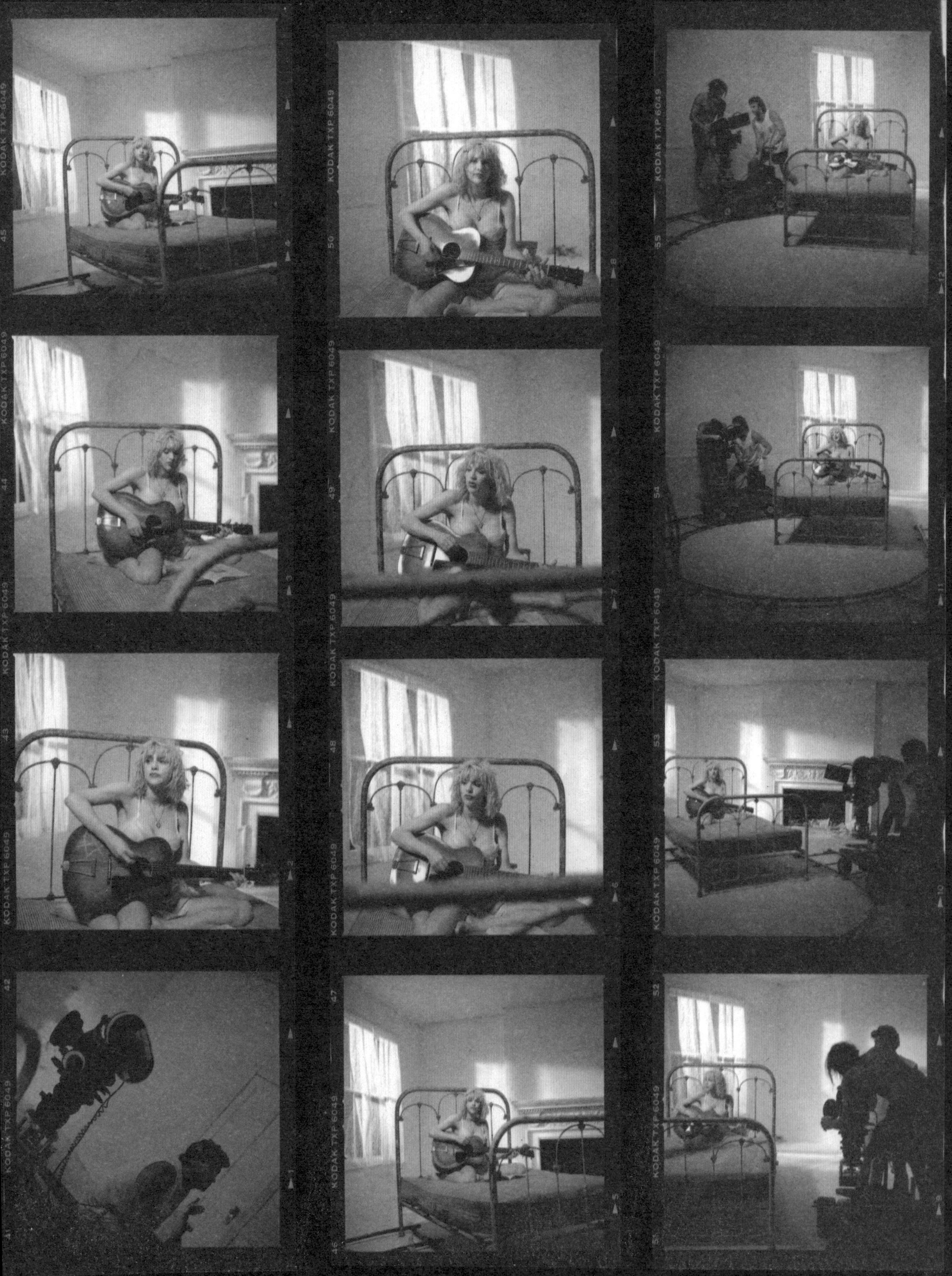
KODAK TXP 6049

Doll Parts

I am
Doll Eyes
Doll Mouth
Doll Legs

I am
Doll arm
Blue veins
Dog Beg
yeah they really want you
"
they really want you they really do
yeah they really want you ..
i do too.
x i want to be the girl w/the most cake
he only loves those things because he loves to see them break
I fake it so true
i am beyond fake. And someday you will ache like i ache
x I am Doll parts
bad skin
Doll heart
(K) stands for knife
For the rest of
my life.

NO PARKING ANYTIME
SODA
ICE CO
ITALIAN
HEROS
SHISH KeBOB
ON THE CO
POPCORN Cotton Candy
SHISH-KA-BOB-ICE CREAM
ITALIAN SAUSAGE-SHISH-K
COTTON CANDY LOLLY POPS
JELLY APPLES ICE COLD DRINKS
KABOB
ITALIAN SAUSA
Budweiser
BEER
Style

lite
&
MGD
ATURN6

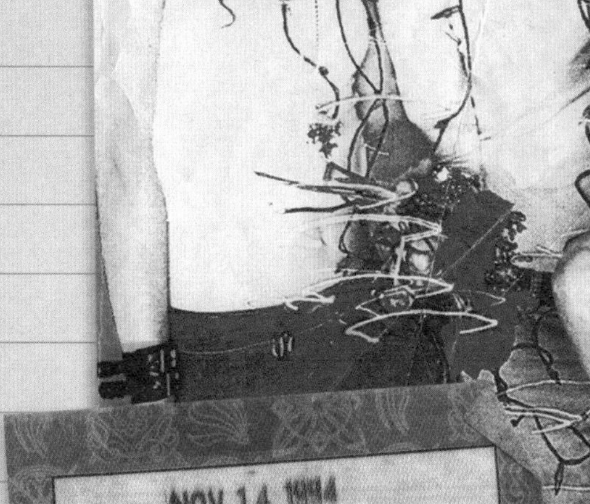
NOV 14 1994
Hole
ALL

SATURDAY NIGHT

THE MARK

NEW YORK

my Body the hand
Grenade.

MADISON AVENUE AT EAST 77TH STREET, NEW YORK, NEW YORK, 10021
TELEPHONE (212) 744-4300 FACSIMILE (212) 744-2749

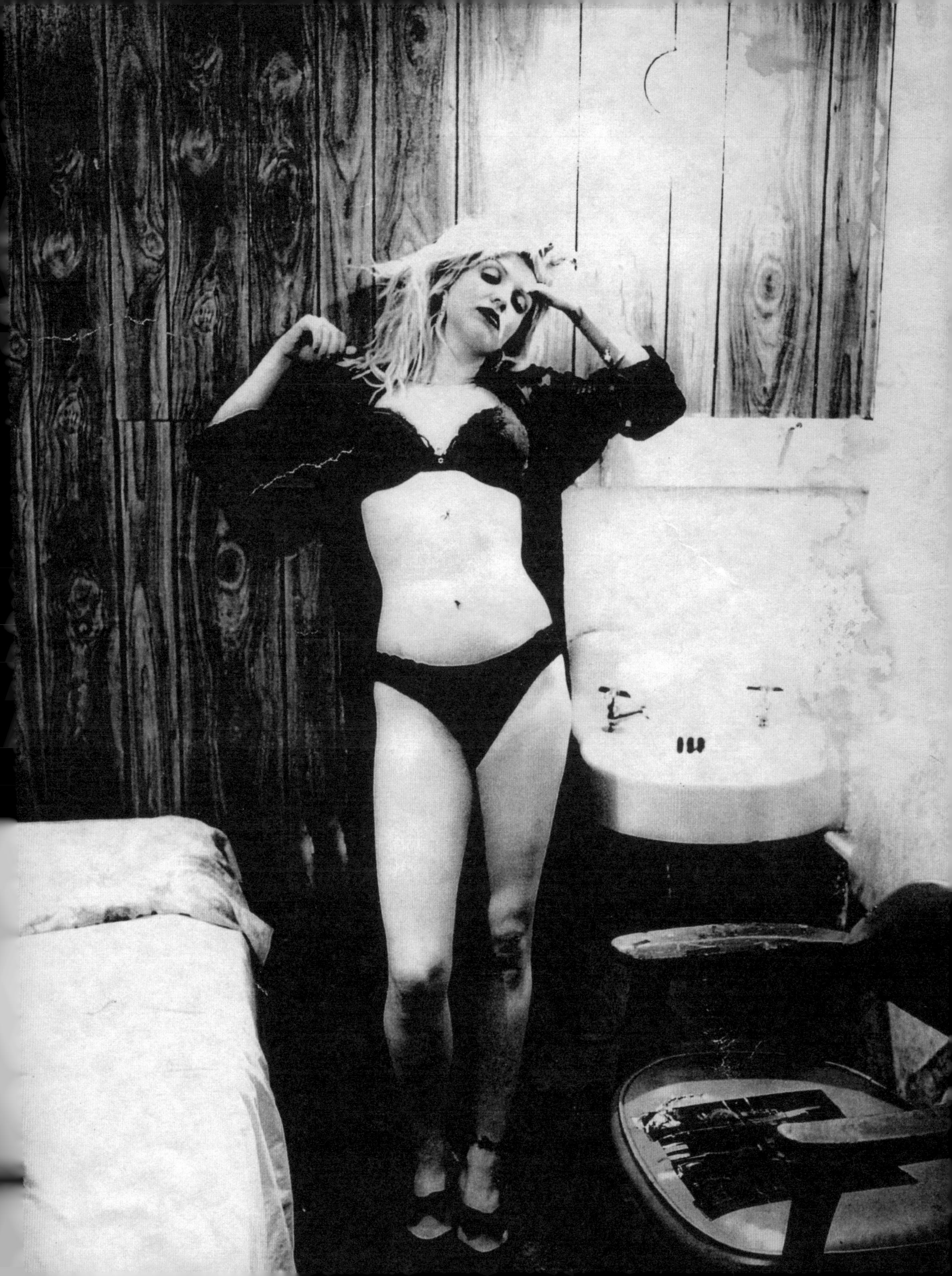

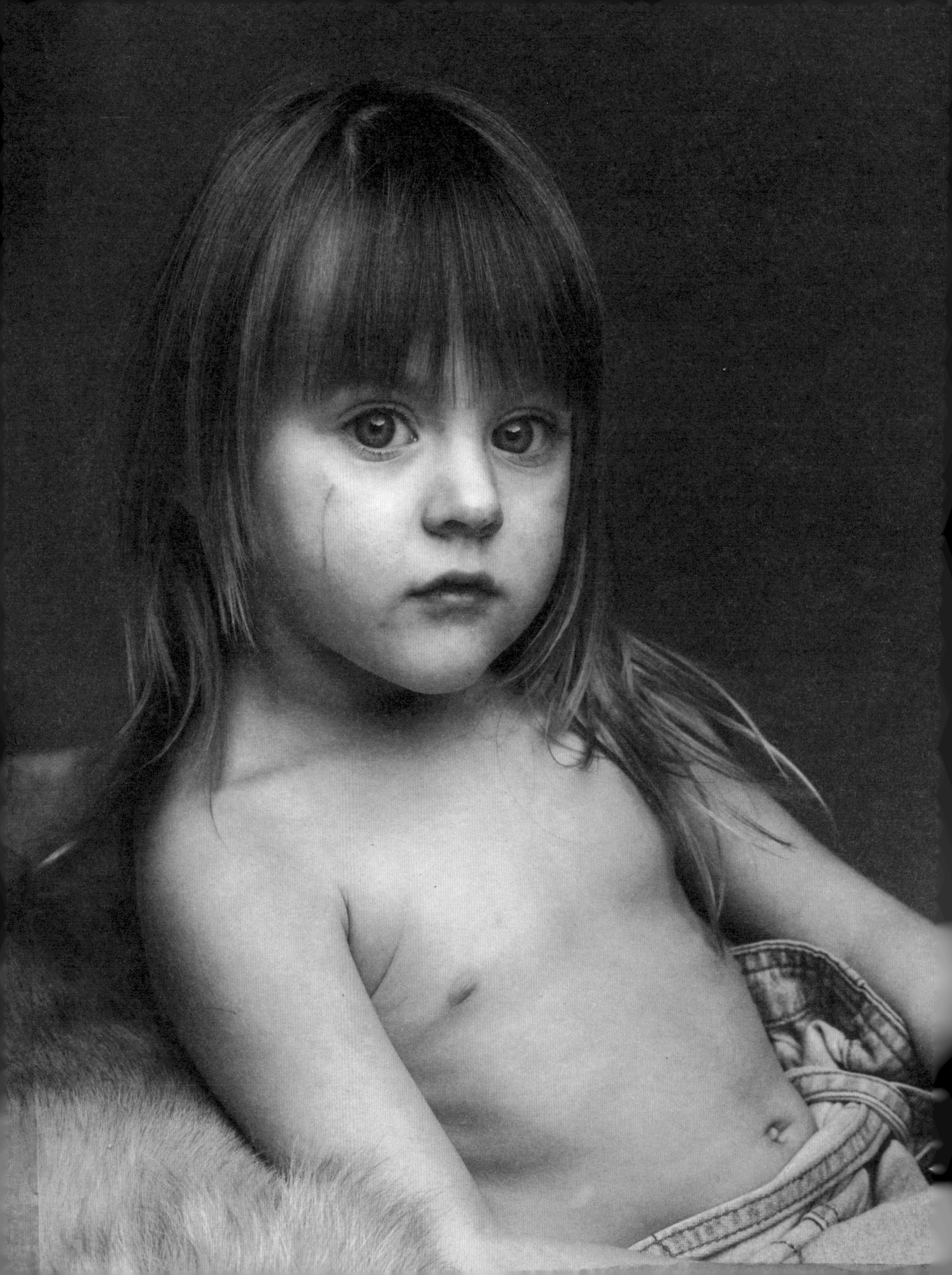

Present!
Not a life lived.
Not a life lived.
Frances Grounds me
her beautiful funny gorgeous
Spirit makes me cry.
her minitrue body
is delightful her love
her atrageous maturity
her sparkling crackling
blue eyes
her fathers Absurdist theatre
her own sense of self
Frances is my life

Someday i hope to make her
So proud and so happy —
my honey girl
with Frances i am here
Right NOW.
i dreamt of hemp.

Oh Frances grow lush and
Strong long limbed
Grow into presence and truth
Grow in the light
my darling girl, my darling
baby girl. ♡

i see you
you are Gods
own child

Reasons to be Beautiful.

I dont want to go
" " anymore
its so dreany and so dull
Squashed the blossom
dropped it on its head
Squashed the blossom
and the blossoms dead

10 good reasons to stay
10 good reasons I cant find
Chorus

Baby take it all the way
taste it anyway
then throw it up

Oh i will
make myself so beautiful
and everything
will be Baught & sold
Give me a reason to
be beautiful
oh Give me Joy
one reason to
To sell my
soul

listen to
what they say
you kill your heart
you fade away
its better to rise
than fade away
its better rise
like an
angel rise like
angel
saw him
rise him like
twisted deformed
some angel
burnt black
for

Dec 15 97

Looking at pictures from Liverpool
How sad it makes me seeing this
Old Bunnymen book.

Les started up the bass line, Will began playing a tinny and repet
style guitar riff, and Ian McCulloch stared shortsightedly at a sh
the lyrics on. The song was 'I Bagsy Yours', a primitive ve
t the small audience didn't realise was that this was
they intended to make it last. Fifteen minut
the drum box off, and for ten second
use.
to Les. "That was to
ion. Oth

getme. i always stand up Survivor my dreaming Rocknard I reach to strangle my own

in the Corner, i reach for my shoes for my feet, everything reasonable finally defeat. it never came!

Sunset Marquis

its all disease
I cannot reach into that place so cold in you
so frozen with pain and with
being fucked.
I am looking at a window
Facing a Room of humiliations and degradations.
those cigarette burns
I know you wonder.....
i needle myself
i see a beautiful mysterious perfect Madonna
Standing next to Joan Jett in an Orioles uniform.
who gave birth to someone
who has affected me so so so profoundly
and what can I do
my eyes are locked in cages
my mouth is never in the right place
my heart is jumping from knees
to Freezer
I can only kiss away your darkest day
I take it upon myself
I wish i wasnt born deformed
I hate my past I hate the grotesque vulgarity
I am.
You shine a pure light into my soul
I see a path so unfettered
I have no second thoughts.
I am carving out Love as though i never know
what it was.
beyond Euphoria & craving & Lust
beyond Loyalty & that ultimate irony, honesty,
I want to build a Love that is God the Lion

DEFEAT
DEFEAT
DEFEAT
DEFEAT

What was bad back then
all the hands strangle
What was bad back then
is still bad now

Now were got poor Diana
w/ her hands
down her
throat

Foam of
a Scapegoat.
in the FORM of a scapegoat

Burn the Witch
with the brokenback

If i was a
princess
i think
id just
gloat

Diana has
scabs on
the sides of
her thumbs
and
potassium
stains
on her
teeth
and
Electrolyte
gin
blossoms
poor thing
Stomp yr
tiara off
Give it

Dontask me what (and yr friends) all
to do with your demons

Crash and burn
all the stars explode tonight
oh its so pretty
~~stars so pretty bright~~
All the lights lay down and died

under such heavy sedation
and in your grip I feel my end
I hope you get well soon
how'd you get so desperate
Slay the World with just one
song

burned the fire from yr eyes
how'd you get so desperate
how'd yr stay alive

HATRED
JEALOUSY
CONFLICT.

Cover Version Celeb Skin

Skin

oh make me over
im all i wanna be
a walking study
in Demonology
yeah now you really made it
so glad you have made it

~~here she comes yeah~~
~~somebody's daughter~~
~~drink it up yeah~~
~~its holy water~~

oh look at my face my name & is might have been
my name is never was
old & her (my names) forgotten

~~stepped on lovers~~

hey now you really made it
so glad you could make it
theres only us left now

you better watch out
what you wish for
it better be worth it
or you could die for it

when i wake up in my make up
its too early for that dress
now im fadeding / ~~wilted & fading~~
somewhere in Hollywood

the Fires gone out
" "

She rides from me twisted
I can barely see her
from my safe fog
but its cold in here
my Fires got out
and where am I anyway
Show me the girl whos gonna die for you
but every child here just cries for you
til the Fire goes out

yeah and where am I?
on he hit so hard it
I saw he hit so
hard I found God

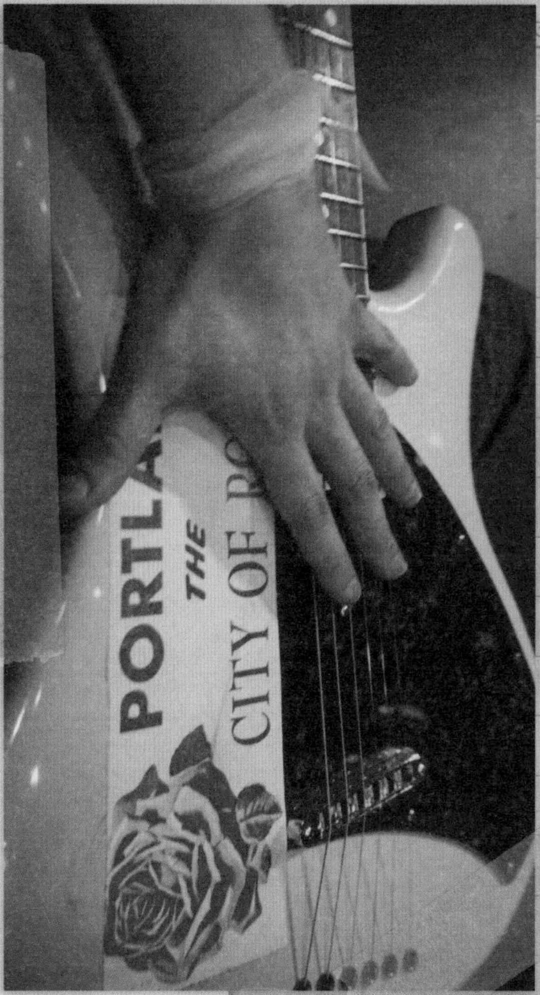

Petals

Youre the angel on
top of the tree
Please come down
Your going to fall on me
Lillies come alive in your hands
the flowers are on fire in your promised land

tear the petals off of you
and make you tell the truth & tear the petals off of you
X never knew how much i wanted you
your the grace of this world your too pure
you kiss the night until the milky way comes loose
tear the petals off of you

ahh its all my mine
help its all mine
I never knew what i could be

all the darling buds of may
they fall with no sound
they fall with no sound
they carry you down

all the lillies bloom & blossom
-
- you too pure for this world
- this world is war
a whore

Absolute
Treasury

& they say they never fade
then they wilt and are forgotten
oh I never loved them anyway
didnt want them

tear the petals
off of me
you are all
ill ever
be

I never
loved
you
anyway

Candy
The poison milk of human kindness
we will get our just desserts
the sour milk of human kindness
we will get just what we did deserve,

I Love; Frances, You, LA, New York, Seattle, Money. generating income. my hair blonde.

I Love being famous.
I Fucking Enjoy it so much.
Why DO I have to explain that?
Because noone else has it. Because its a fight. Because its psychicly Charging.
Hey, Because I get off on it.

I Love playing music;
its the best thing ever. I give it what noone Else does and I feel so wired when someone is competing with me or pushing me; especially when its my own self.
Because it affords me the power to feel that I am worth something. In order to DO IT RIGHT I would renounce just about anything.

Gangsta Rap Gets Spanked in Congress
SPIN
COURTNEY LOVE COMES CLEAN
On Axl Rose, Eddie Vedder, and Herself
By Dennis Cooper
VANILLA ICE
Oh God, He's Back
COUNTING CROWS
Bland Guys Finish First
RADIO CLASH
The FCC vs. Stephen Dunifer
BLOOD SPORT
Kickboxing
By William T. Vollmann
Plus:
Nine Inch Nails
John Waters
Rubén Blades
Superchunk
MAY 1994 $2.95
CAN$3.50/UK£2.25

Linear thinking does not Come naturally to me moreover it kills my imagination. Nothing happens. No bell rings no moment of

Here and Now.

No moment that says Yes.

Without those moments I am not alive. and so, rather than driving at a goal, I like so much better to go thru' a spiral

i would like to go back to school (Columbia) and study theology and One hard science and will someday when my Victory Garden is Grown and i develop a fantastic hybrid Frances ~~Cobain~~ Farmer Rose fat as a baby fist and sundappled amber with tea rose climbing Qualities. F.C. roses are my Goal of legacy (in keeping w/ Whitman and with Yeats). God bless you and Dr Bronner. Essene. Essene. one world.

Sunburst. a greenhouse providing real orchids to the Northwest. i want her on cello. astronomer and NYU Graduate. oh well She toddles with joy delight and perfection. she toddles with pink and lovely smell i only speak of this love with K! but i am overjoyed for you. Bliss.

God bless. Merry Merry.

Your formerly precocious and now just pretentious friend. in Soul.

Courtney.

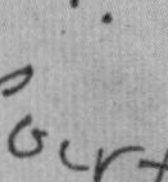

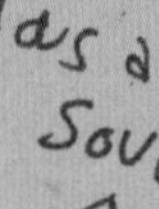

P.S. you will cry and cry. Joy you have never known. i promise.

these are private

the makeup makes me

oh baby pretty so polite
pretty pretty fight or flight

put on the makeup you've got stuff to sell
put on the makeup to cover up the hell.

and the ladies at the counter say
this perfume blows you away
this very color is of the hour
this little tube gives you infinite power

and the ladies at the counter yell
let this bra! push up your hell!

lotion potion i can gleam
move like a well oiled machine
Glitter & Glamour it's got to hide
all the Rest I hide inside —
because the makeup makes me — be

the mirror keeps on lying.
and I keep on trying –

Breathe in the fire
that destroyed the man
hell hath no fury like the Master plan
dangerous Girls in bloom
Coming into this room
naked on their face –
her finger on the trigger
the trigger of this world
You can shut up the lady
but you cannot stop the Girl
her finger on the trigger
Shes got her heart in
mind
Will she ever find the Right one
with her trigger heart this
time.

*f means polemic or Claim

Polemic chick history →

1896 Alice Guy
The Cabbage Fairy
French
p (First Fictional film)

1906

Elvira Notari → 60 features
100 docus

1913 Olga Wohlbruck – German f. director
1915 Julia Ivers GM of Bosworth, Inc.
a studio.

Viola Lawrence Editor
Lois Weber highest paid f. of silent era

*

1916
Anita Loos subtitle writing
Mary Pickford first Production Company
Lois makes a movie
'the dumb Girl of Portici'
with stars Pavlova –
(want to see
This is my cineaste phase.....

1920 L. Gish directs the all F. production
of Remodeling her husband.

1927 Thea Von Harbou writes Metropolis
29 Arzner directs the
Wild Party

P → [illegible] (invents the
boom on a fishing
pole)

62 VERA Chytilova Czech ask Milos
Femme

73 Pamela Douglas black producer
Universal

53 Ida – the Hitcher writer

59 Marguerite Duras writes screenplay
for Hiroshima Mon Amour
(where is it)

79 Gillian My brilliant career 88 Penny - Big
82 Seidelmann Smithereens 93 Campion wins for Piano
86 Donna Deitch Desert hearts 98 Lisa Cholodenko High art
I still love kind hearts & coronets. I love Alec Guinness. sexy.

August 18th
2999

Shes turning seven; i think i've seen what they mean by Heavenly.

Shes so gorgeous. Shes so beautiful. & Shes mine!

Frances C.B Cobain I Love you

Shoulders and good health
like her
genius Complicated
nutty mummy.

her MUMA'S ♡ was
Tough to Everyone else
in the world.
MUMA said "let Em all
get the hell away if
they try to hurt my little
girl"

There was a
beautiful diamond
eyed baby
with crystal blue
eyes like her
beautiful daddy
and Strong →

DONT EVER  FUCK WITH ME

DAUGHTER

my little Girls the only
one in this world
Skin like a blue moon
Dancing on Black Pearls
my little Girls got Genes
She can whip your ass at anything & y'all ~~she'll~~ never be good enough.

Shes fragile as Glass
tougher than diamonds,
~~[illegible]~~ Shes wall to wall Class,
~~[illegible]~~ & rockn rolls Queen

i play the witch over & over
Im a great fighter
But Im the worlds greatest mother.
my little Girl is a Lion
with a touch that could raise the dead
Shes brilliant rare & she defines the word kind
She inhabits the Empathy
She inherited the wind. the clouds. the sky. the trees.
She inherited Eyes that see everything
but one day one of you will try to take her away
the beauty the eyes the money the name
my baby swims in the deep end of the pool
the pearls & Rubies wont get to that Girl

She rides like Thunder stops on a dime
Dances the Sugar Plum fairy better than Ballanchine
Knows when an Earthquake's coming.
She speaks with the dead.
& her daddy is gone, I'll always be the fire
that surrounds the big hug she needs from anyone
Who'd use her, my baby seen Chery blossom Rain.
& she feels way too much.
She feels your fucking pain.
I block your pain out.
your Greedy & Slezy. I wish i was a prosecutor.
my speciality would be honar.
but my full time Job is called.

Tell me what to do
Cuz I'll do anything.
Tell me when I'm thru
Cuz you'll do anything.....

Nothing
you do is at it
seems
No part of
You will
Ever be
Clean.
Ever Ever
Ever be Clean.

pg. 208 / /

Ive been driven to a perfume Factory in Grasse.
If I dont make the Greatest perfume I will have nothing.
I walk through a field of Jasmine into the back
door of a house / Factory. Theres a huge room with Every
smell imaginable in Glass vials. I look for Neroli. I have
to make a perfume out of Neroli - Sand -
hummingbird feathers -
Cognac

petrified wood Amber & seahorse.
thats the Secret recipe and its
impossible so I give up after
making smell after smell that
doesnt work.
I spot a harpsichord in the Corner
dusty & old

I sit at it and begin to play.
I write a song called 'Mary Lied'
its easy and delicate to write
it comes to me fast, and I can
play harpsichord very well.
all the cats in the house
come sit by
the harpsichord with me.
theres about 30 cats or more.
they all love the song.

Take this Glitter thing
& just do it til it DIES....

I look at the clock.
If I dont make the perfume soon
I will lose everything
my house, my love, etc.
by a miracle theres
a jar with ground up seahorse
in it I sort of
slosh together Neroli-Seahorse and some bitter rare red
berry flowers. I smell it – the music has restored my
sense of smell. its not what I had in mind but I
realize it will do. I tuck the vial in my bra
and walk back out to the jasmine
field.

Its nothing to be proud of.
I wanted in And I wanted in bad.
Sometimes Id think When the
Sub pop thing was happening
"Fuck it. Im going to wash
Sunset Blvd Clean. Me. Im
Going to Find the Four Best
Female players on Earth under
25 And fuck shit up
and stay RIGHT HERE in
LA like the peppers or Jane's
Do and watch the hairbands
go.
Hairbands and numetal is
the Exact same thing

Even in Juvenile hall in Eugene
Id seen the back of Nancy Wilsons
Fender flash lights as heart who
were 2 women basically one
who played Page leads in kicky
boots I could see Everything.
In Autzen Stadium.
& the Month before Robert "Chino"
Towne had been there filming
"Personal Best" and people kept
yelling "Check the gate"
and "Action" and Instead
"Personal Best" out my window.

So it hadnt been so bad For me.
But I had to Conform just as much
as Kurt and I had to play ball
Just the same.

the only thing I had was cool hair
and better lyrics than anybody
Else. And a Really Bad Reputation.

the only thing he had was Genius.
and he was beautiful. and he
could play a Guitar just like
Ringing a bell.

and so the ~~assholes~~ the
Rich Assholes who were
Running Everything now let us
Both in.

You could be Brad pitt and Julia Roberts
put together and It still is not as
powerful as Beautiful music.
Being a film actor is cool.
Especially if your a guy filmactor like
Edward or Russell Crowe.
Then you really get to Fuckaround.
It's called being a "leading Characteractor"
like Robert Deniro.
But its still nowhere as Powerful as
writing these Beautiful songs
Everybody a certain age Remembers
where they were the First time they
heard teen spirit on the Radio.
It was the opposite feeling of the
Some people three years Later hearing
that my husband had shot himself
in the head with a Shotgun.

And so the Power Kurt brought
to Everyone around him was so
messive, but kurt himself was
very Queit to others. he didn't
want people to know him. and when
we started to go out we knew we were
in Love when one night maybe the
Third night we crossed that little
Bridge by the Beverly Gardens Hotel
in the valley, and he said "i wish
i was more like you" and he
meant it and i looked at him
& thought about the fact that he
Really broke Chads drums almost
Every night. He was not Conservative
like me and i said "i wish i was
more like you" and I really meant it

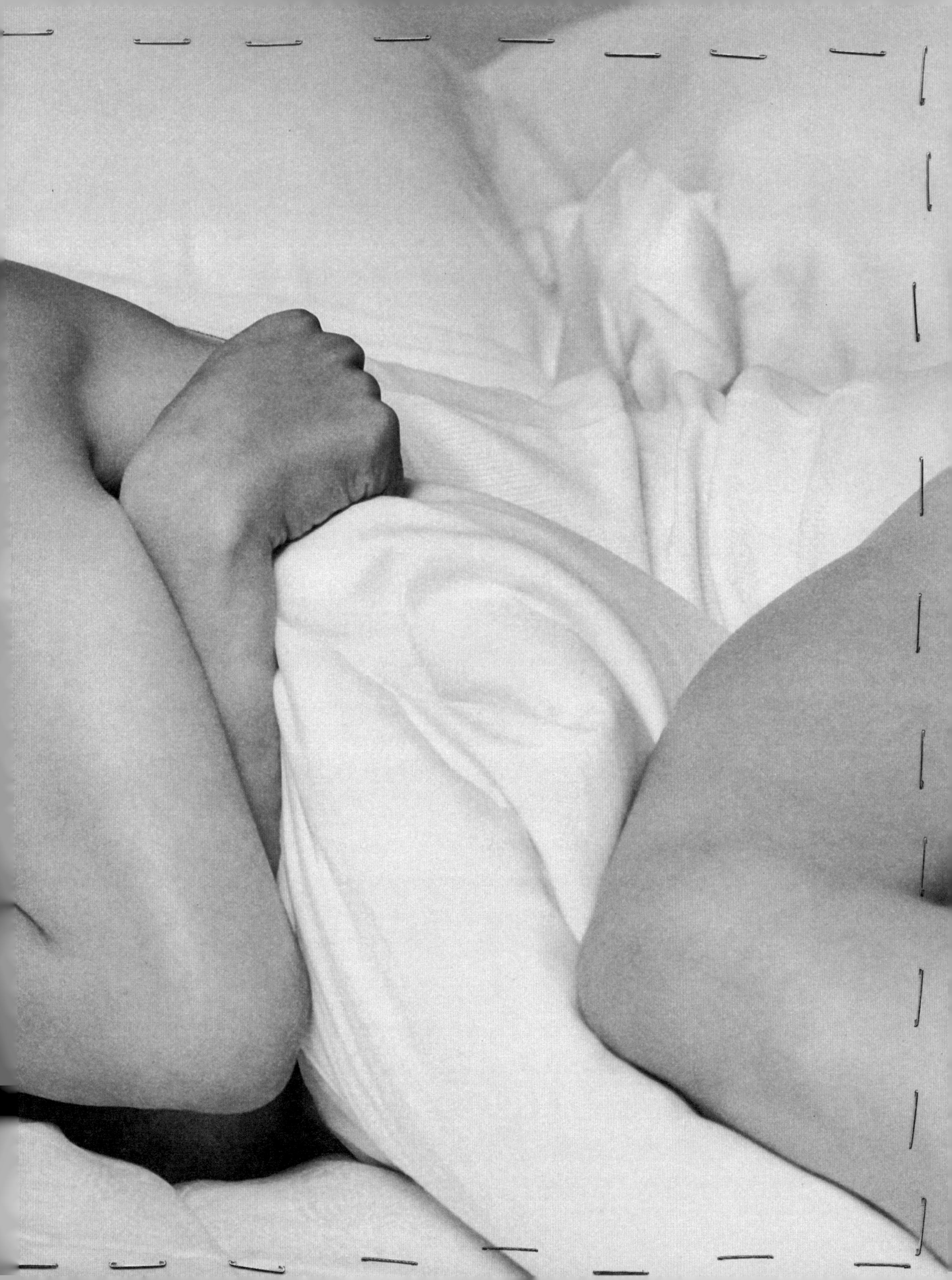

pg. 214 / /

June 30, 2002.

MARC JACOBS

Dear Courtney,

I am equally touched and moved by both the beautiful gift, and the kind note you sent me.

I will always keep this extraordinary, personal gift to myself – private!, as you said. It will never be shared with anyone else – I give you my word that I will not betray your kindness and your generosity in any way – ever.

You mentioned that I have always been sweet and funny to you – That has been easy for *me* as I have always been awestruck by your style, your intelligence and your talent.

I guess now, I feel completely blown away by your sensitivity as well.

Again, thank you very much,
With all my love,
Marc.

NASHVILLE
MAY 99

HOUSTON THEATRE
May 9.99

Blue tubeSkirt
Blue Suede top. LINC.

*EXAMPLES OF SHOW LOOKS.
FROM VARIOUS VENUES.

Sounds leather
hand ripped by
US

[redacted] wrong coat.
[redacted]
This is Jil Sander.

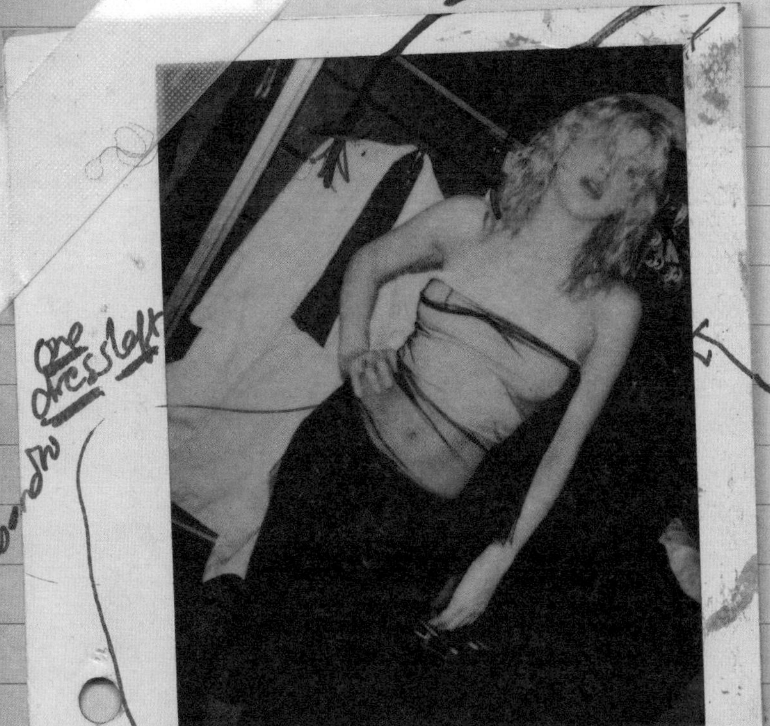

Alessandro.
in Washington

Del Aqua

Gave to ~~[illegible]~~ ~~[illegible]~~ Jeffrey

Beige knit

Also Gave one

ok I give in
will you leave me alone
If I say nothing
worth the truth it may be hell down there
but its heaven up here

She walks by on a stick, she looks so ~~[illegible]~~ soul sick
I cant drive I cant drive
Its the kindness of strangers that keeps me
alive

and i see the desert once
grown into a film dont ask me Im a Gilded

whore of the realm

the porno burns
into the sweet

a hole
tooth You call your soul

and In the night we all
stay home
Except for us who are
never alone

Oh I'm PREACHING!
I'm PREACHIN!!
TOO BAD I'M NOT GOING TO HEAVEN!!

GUN

~~Fight~~ club for Girls

Shoelwragig

venus of willendorf

We have a virus.
it's a strain lain dormant
for thousands of years - for ever
it pokes up now & again
& through the prism of a
hundred thousand refracted
beams of poisonous lights
is distorted & twisted
to be something that it is not.
It gets slandered, it gets shattered
punished burned at the stake
drowned and made a humiliating
example of - over and over
again.
The "Virus" will 'ruin' our society
the 'Virus' will certainly cause
change within our society

and that will not do.....
This is the virus of Queens, of Divas,
of Prima Donnas, of Amazons,
of Hilary. of the Matriarchy.
Proud, Graceful, full of power.
This is the "Virus" that tells me
deep in my brainstem that I
can be whatever it is that I want to be.
the 'Virus' that never understood

growing up why there werent female baseball teams or protaganists worth thier salt in Comic books or Video Games of my Gender.
The intention to gain ~~do~~ a straight up, Square, linear objective such as writing a record, writing a poem, getting involved in my Community getting involved in femmeniste Causes, even something Simple such as attending to the Everyday Common Conceptual art of Celebrity

always seems to get perverted twisted distorted.
I see my words in Interviews and so rarely are those words what I said, how I said it, what I meant.
I look on Interviews as a way of sharing information, particularly womens magazine interviews, a way of saying Look at this cool thing I found (because I'm always searching for Cool things to make me a better, happier person) and it generally seems to Come out all wrong, twisted the rebel grrrl, the weird sister. There she goes.
and there is certainly some of that Rebel & wierd in who I am and what I do

But we all have the virus.
we all have the Secret Amazon
virus in us. that much i know
for sure.
Some ~~people~~ women treat thier
Celebrity with a solemnity best
saved for funerals. This can be valid
if one uses it nonstop (as W. Ryder)
for good causes.
I cant take it too seriously no
matter how hard i try.
Because number one, it doesnt
have much to do with my art.
If I work and apply what
many people have described as
a Calvinist work ethic and I
pay attention to my spirit
and the purity of what I'm doing
my music, my writing, my acting &
now producing

Those things will come out well.
Those things will not be cheap or
haphazard or "pop" – I dont do
pop (in art), I just dont know how.
But Celebrity *is* cheap.
I hate to break it to everyone as
its, I'm sure a billion(s) dollar
Industry on some level, but what is
it? taking lots of pictures and
using the media as a way of
selling your products, and in the
meantime getting projected on by
thousands or millions of people.
Theres only one thing to do with it.
Spread the Virus.
Yet Everytime I try, in womens
magazines in any case,
My words get distorted and poisoned.
I think a clacque of Editrixes

have assigned me honorary bad
girl the same way theyre assigned, say,
meg Ryan Miss Spunkygirl,
I have seen Ms. Ryan Eyes in
a trance in mismatched socks and
a cool mans suit standing on
the side of a stage in Central park
watching Patti Smith and mouthing

Every Single lyric (Patti Smith
being someone who has the virus,
lives the virus, and can be used
as a touchstone for anyone
of us that needs to access the
virus)

A REAL GIRL ROCKSTAR

1. is glamarous
2. starts trends
3. Makes Entrances & Exits that are BIG.
4. has a twinkle of Fun in the eye.
5. has a twinkle of Evil in the eye
6. has listened to patty smiths "PISS FACTORY" many many times
7. Starts a hairdo.
8. is nice to all crew. (or your a to bitch)

a POISED thankyou with eye contact.

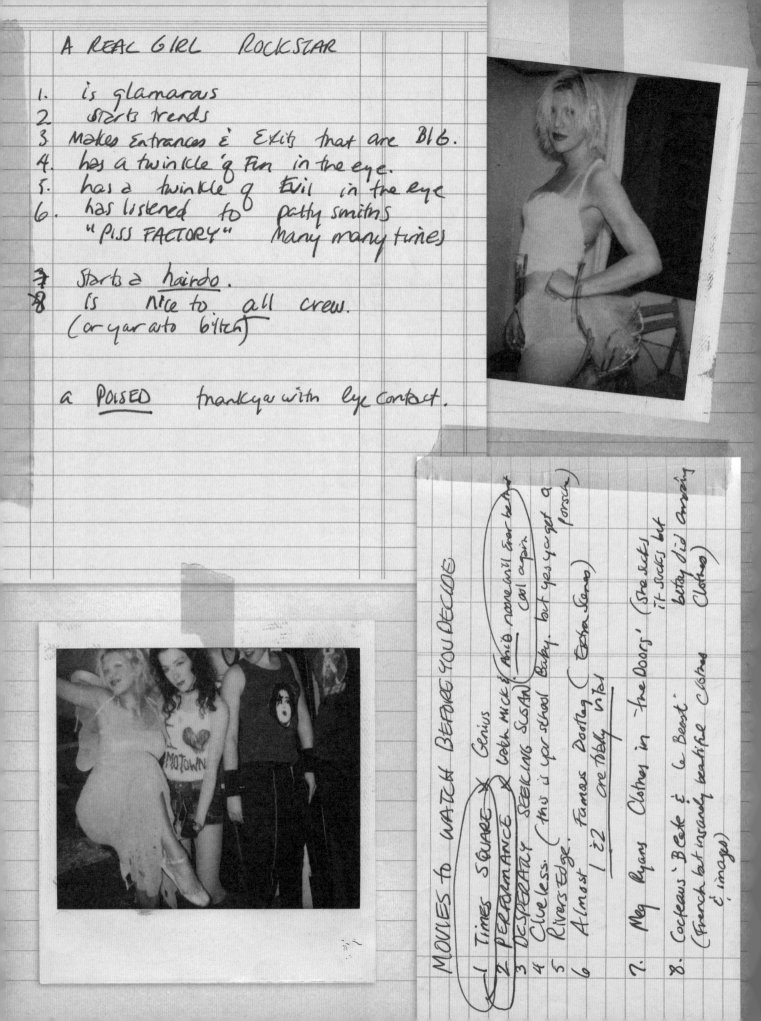

MOVIES to WATCH BEFORE YOU DECIDE

1 Times SQUARE ✗ Genius
2 PERFORMANCE ✗ watch Mick & Anita noone will ever be that cool again
3 DESPERATLY SEEKING SUSAN
4 Clueless. (this is your school Baby. but yes you get a porsche)
5 Rivers Edge.
6 Almost Famous Bootleg (Extra Scenes)
1 & 2 are totally vital

7. Meg Ryans Clothes in 'the Doors' (she sucks it sucks but betsy did amazing Clothes)

8. Cocteaus 'Belle & la Beast' (French but insanely beautiful Clothes & images)

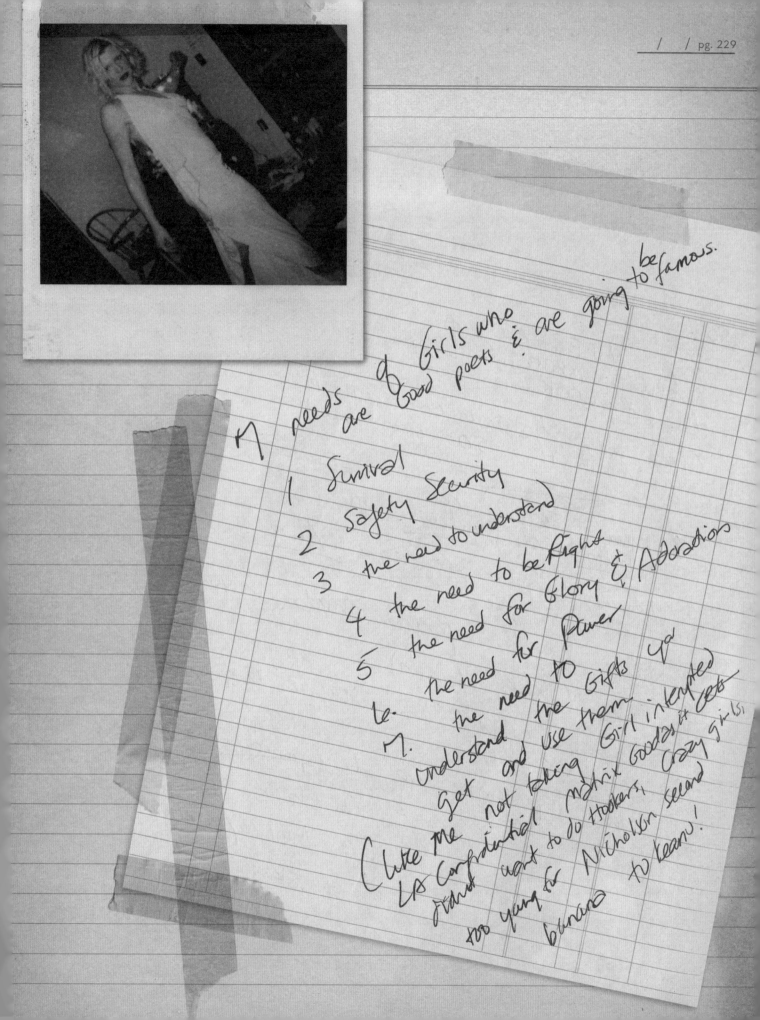

My needs are of Girls who are Good poets & are going to be famous.

1 Survival
Safety Security
2 the need to understand
3 the need to be Right
4 the need for Glory & Adoration
5 the need for Power
6. the need to
7. the need to understand the Gifts ya Get and use them

(like me not taking Girl interrupted
LA Confidential matrix Good as it Gets
stand want to do Hookers, Crazy girls,
too young for Nicholson second
banana to keanu!

Black Guitar is #3

1 Kiss kiss
2. Bang Bang
3 Gash slash BANG OOPS!

heart
Exploding
Black/silver &
lotsared Guitar

kitty with a lit
match.

VBerndt? or someone way better
~~[illegible]~~ 2) the one thing i saw
sucked so

call JOE MAMA!
& give VB another shot

this should be a big
ol' exploding
heart.

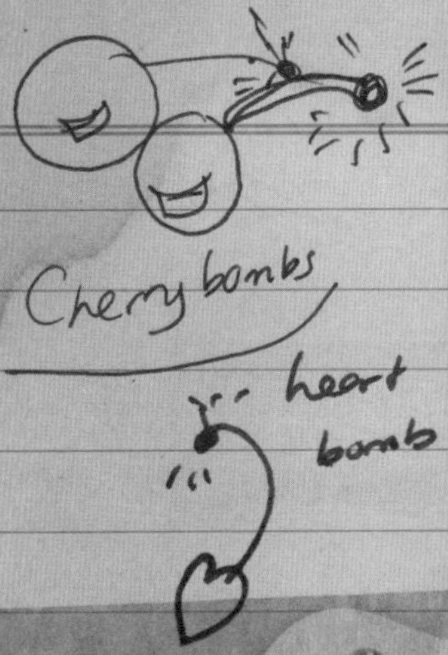

MAJOR SCALES b

1. GOVERNED BY 4th
2. FLAT THE 4th
3. RETAIN THE FLATS

O	C	D	E	F	G	A	B	C	
	ROOT	WS	WS	HS	WS	WS	WS	HS	
	1st	2nd	3rd	4th	5th	6th	7th	8th	OCTAVE
1	F	G	A	Bb	C	D	E	Fb	
2	Bb	C	D	Eb	F	G	A	Bb	
3	Eb	F	G	Ab	Bb	C	D	Eb	
4	Ab	Bb	C	Db	Eb	F	G	Ab	
5	Db	Eb	F	Gb	Ab	Bb	C	Db	
6	Gb	Ab	Bb	Cb	Db	Eb	F	Gb	
7	Cb	Db	Eb	Fb	Gb	Ab	Bb	Cb	

Run away your heads on fire
Can't tell the difference
Between hate and desire
Everything went all fucking
Wrong chaos reigns in
This bed, where I'm alone

Fuck you up won't get me out
Wash that stain
Under your skin
Can't wash that really
Nothing to wash it in yeah
Twist that rag under your skin
Can't help yourself
You gonna rub me in, yeah

then well do it Again
& you'll deny it to all your
friends.
I have be come the End.
I have be come Revenge

Do it Again BP

REVENGE
leave me

All my love is in vain
Can't abide by this pain
All my love's been blood
Don't have enough
Can't mend broken heart
House has fell apart

Spacey tried to get me booted
from the
Old Vic.
Elton
told him
to fuck
off.
I always
knew
Elton
was a
saint.
plus
I
upstaged
Acey
anyway

me & milos in bed.
I LOVE YOU MILOS FORMAN!!

Ribcosa fabric
Less length in front more behind
But a fanny Girdle from hell
saw

People die in New York

Im shattered
So im always Right
and thru
the CRACK
Can you see my light?
If you can
Then maybe im
Crazy as they say
Stoned & dying Blind
i crawling up your legs
Like a fuck-me vine
People Die in New York.
alone.
in the night.

But i want to have the best ass as i
Grind Glass
and the moment has

less than 14 hours previous
a Bitchy stewardess from Bransons airline
had me ARRESTED. Richard a very sweet man
is apologising.

writing is an intimacy i dont like. i feel forced into it. you can now see my mind working. you think you know me. you can then imagining i can make the revolution simply by changing my own life

jihad
the mother of all

Violate me more with your "knowledge" of my mind / heart.

In a patriarchal society men identify themselves with culture and women, w/ nature and the body

i am a Public figure unhappy with my share of the American dream. There can only be one reason for this. I am on drugs and have the morals and mentality of a cartoon character. what did i want after all?? If i wanted certain things, like respect and privacy i should have put out certain universal female symbols like Chastity and Ethereal mutedness, like making nice with Daddy like standard issue demure sullen chic. in a Caste hierarchy we are comforted by the idea of one "marrying "up." Us girls can use our wits, looks or dumbluck to get us out of the concil flat / waitress job and get us rolling around on tightly threaded Italian linen.

·Demonization.

Oct 10th

we all get olde. we all fade away.
our lights all get dim. we all lock
our doors. we all get greedy.
we all hide behind a collective
moral mediocrity. i want the goodness
Inside of me to shine. INFRASTRUCTURE! NOW!

This is A GAMBLERS GAME.
WATCHED "DIG!" AGAIN
1. TO "ONJI": TO PASSIVELY STAND BY & NOT
HELP A DYING human being
2. I think i hate rocknroll
3. one more stand - sexy sexy arming
monkey. make it real.
make it right.
toast it to myself
name for baby. xxxx

they have stripped me of my
my lifeblood
energy have taken from me everything

NOV 16

I had a great talk with
Frances on the phone.
Shes so wanted by me.
I hate the patronizing
attitude people have
toward her. She does too.
good fucking luck. I love her
so totally completely &
utterly. its total & fierce.
Shes my blood & my lifeline.
She was always a golden child.
always snuggled & loved up
& wanted. I guess this is
the middle passage of my life
she got really upset when I let
myself go. so did I. who doesn't.

Deceased like my Grandmother did

Broke rockstar to
become Worlds !!!
Richest woman!!!

Broke Rockstar to become
Worlds Richest woman......

as a consequence of
never receiving any
love from my mother.

as a consequence of
my Grandmothers
ice floe.

Big Glamourous things happened
to me_

Big Glamourous things ~~happened~~
to my baby doll little bean.

& i wanted you
like noone ~~else~~ before
Said you coming back for me
honey

~~This is how troubles born now~~
honey

This is how ~~troubles born~~
hell forms

This is how a storm begins
This is how troubles born
Listen to how she screams
Listen to her wail
You've Given birth to terrible things
now watch them unveil
So I sing the blues
& I sing them true

listen to her twist 
listen to her snake
put the shackles on a little tighter
now you say too late
listen to my torment
listen to my pain
please come on back here
let me try again
& the rain it came down
& the wind it moaned
& she's wrapped in rags so elegant
& she's got no home
& it's spectacular
to watch her fall so hard
& when you stab her
can you hear me crying
you you can stab a little harder
sharpen that knife

Oh baby stab a little harder
we've got the rest of my life

The devil made

Na na na na na
~~now you a knife~~
your devil
heart
your devil
doll
Na na na nana nana

Ive got all night

Ive lost my mind
& Ive lost control
& Ive lost the feeling in my arms
& Im a lost soul

make the most of me
Dont spit me out
This is how dirty Girls Get clean
Dont leave me now

CafCGDACDAfem

And ~~she~~'s looking at me
and he looks real dumb
why are you staring
this is how it's done
this is how it screams
this is how it stretches
like a million whiplashes
on all of your bitches

& the night
comes hauling
lonely stars
fell down
not a drop of
mercy in this
whole dry town
& I still want him
he's got what I need
This is how baby dirty girls get clean
What

Listen to her lust ~~it's an~~ angry star
devil heart
~~on your~~ Runs your
Hear her disgrace
Listen to the fragile things
as they all break
Watch from the comfort
the comfort of your home
Listen to her shame come up screaming
Listen to her moan

~~Remai~~ Cf
@ em

I feel so lonely, after my friends and what I've been through. I feel so aching yearning lonely o; no I do not want my diaries published. I want my poetry & lyrics published. I dont want my gobbledegook nonsense "Romantic" cathartic unstable beliefs published.

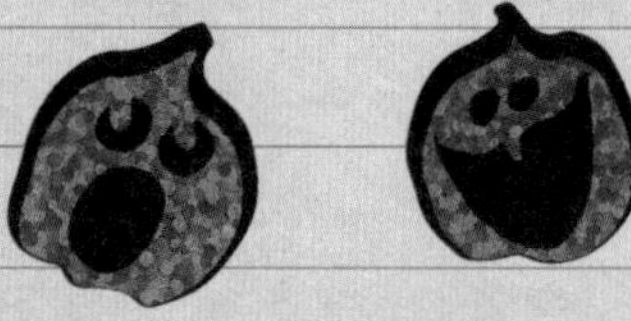

people want to do movies so badly because each part changes the soul. that's the secret. it's not the fame part. that's addictive. it's the harmonic of changing who you are at a soul level. you evolve towards enlightenment faster. it's why experienced film stars are more enlightened Light ened theyre moved through character after character & been filmed from 35 shared mm doing it & it has changed them. I want my growth back. I want to be changed again. it's magical it's so so real!

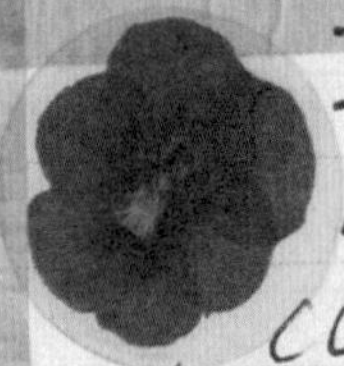

I feel ready for a brand new life now. I've scrubbed clean the mud & rags of 2000-01-02-03-04 & 05. Five years of hell. Everything runs in 7 year cycles. well I'm definitely out of my darkness now.

What We did to me
at the Sunset Marquis
When We left me
in such a state
with no warning
about the people at my gate
When I fell right in
like a stupid Girl
When I slipped & fell & was gone
down on my luck
down at the heels
oh baby you are not the only one
all my secrets come & go
at the Chateau
but for privacy for my reality
I hide behind the walls of the
Sunset Marquis

& for every bad ending
there was a spectacular begining
believe me

dont you bother me
I have my privacy
In my own world at the
Sunset marquis
I can trash my room
I can hit the floor
and they will just take care of me
I can spend Christmas alone
at the Sunset Marquis
and I've been there all my life
dont come here to fuck with me
its the only home that i know
im gonna hide behind the
gates of the Marquis

NOV 31 2005 NOV 31 2005

an old diary of mine from my love affair (marriage surfaced at Sanctuary today. i read it. i miss being loved by a husband very much by my husband there were pictures of Kurt in there. and pictures from the nightmare Vanity Fair photo shoot wich Ruined My life back then. pictures of Kurt walking with William Burroughs. I really miss him.

Follow me down to the Sunset
Marquis, Gamble it all & lose it on me
& whose sorry now. Im sorry now
Inside my room at the Sunset Marquis
we can play rotten neighbours
from bad families
whose your daddy now?
Wheres your daddy now?
Inside the walls of the Sunset Marquis
we can do all the things
that noone believes
people like us do.
heres looking at you.
& I can tell that we are never
going to be friends & I can tell that
this is going to have a bad end &
I dont know who im here to believe
Ill just be thankful If Im breathing
when you leave.

Follow me back to the ~~Sunset Marquis~~
lock all the doors
Ive got something you need
Oh baby you can move.
You can light up a room
& the lights gone obscene
But ~~I~~ you looked real to me
follow me down to my walk of
shame
my dirty little secret has a dirty
little name
& the hookers got loud
But dont tell them now
Follow me back to the Sunset Marquis
play rich n famous n bad royalty
is that what you want?
So insouciant.
Inside the walls of the Sunset Marquis
Ill never tell no it will die with me
oh the things i have seen no it
will die with me.
Follow me back to the Sunset Marquis
we can play rich n famous & live eternally
Ill be at the bar whenever you are

wont you lock yourself in at
the Sunset Marquis
play the part of
absurd ~~royalty~~ parody
is that what
you want?
So insouciant? n

wont you
follow me
back to the
Sunset Marquis
we can do all
the things that
noone believes
that people like us
do
heres looking at you

~~D aed f C D~~
D F C D
D F C D – G

wont you follow me down to the
Sunset marquis we can
play rich n famous n
happy families
n Ill let you down
n youll let me down
we'll burn the place down
yeah down to the Ground

& i can tell that were
here gonna be friends
& i can tell that this
is gonna have a bad end

The Protection of men

within
my lifespan
i never believed i would need
the protection of men—

Cut me, bend me, shape me and
I dont need the
protection of men.
within my wingspan
I dont need the
protection of men

dont stand for me
I dont stand for you.
I will defy you—
even if it means i am
through
Through the finish to the End
How did i end up with the protection of men

If i was a boy
Could i get a bigger room
Could i have a bigger bomb
Could i go to the moon
If i was born a boy
would you just cut me a break
would this hurt so bad, it truly Aches
if i was A boy
if i was a Boy
Could i walk miles & miles away
from this trouble that is keeping me
from this blue that is holding sway
would i be mutilated
humiliated, cursed & fated to grind away my time
with my heart on the line
should have been a boy
all that burnt rule privelegles
building power not burning bridges
throwing down not throwing up
If i dont say it Ill erupt
You wouldnt do it to a boy
you would not do this to a boy

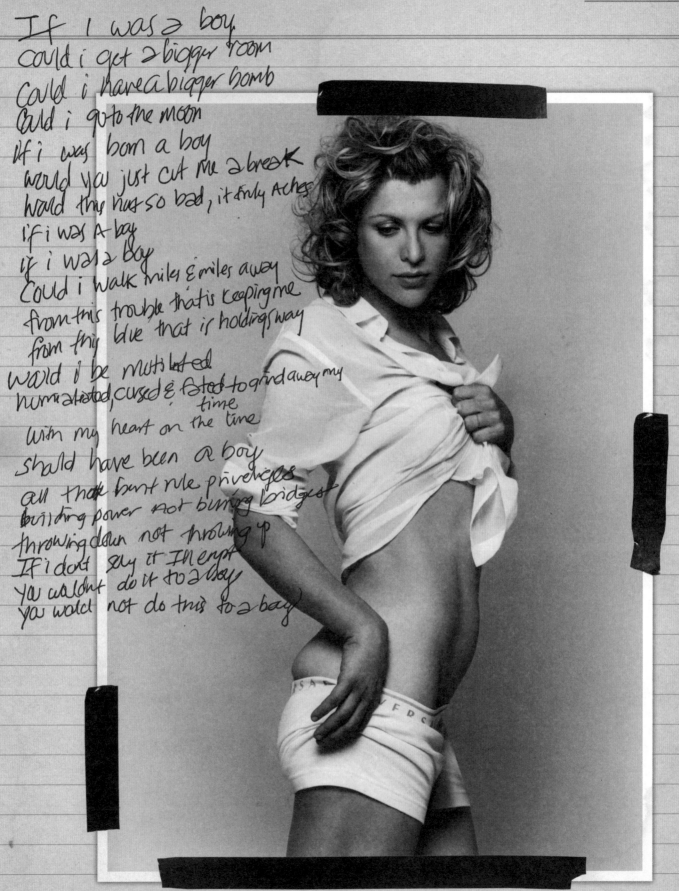

I have never bred a man
& I just dont understand this

you say ~~are~~ you love me more than words
you say you love me more than her
I will have you. & I know you want me. Somewhere deep within
my bedroom walls are caving down
& Everyone can see us now
my bedroom wall are so thin
Can you see me wait for him
my bedroom walls are all in Ruins
You have come Ransacked my Path
My bedroom walls have come to rot
You have Everything I've got
& i need more than my share
Its because I really care
underwhelmed & oversized
Baby what did you expect

Why do I love
this man: hes the first one Ive loved
Kurt style. he Reminds me of Kurt in so many ways.
And i had to chose Kurt for 2.5 years.
I think .... despite Everyone "loathing" him &
he is Golden
worth the pain.

▼ STUDENT ID. NO. AND/OR NAME ▼

Did i bend the rules
Did i shake it up for you
Did i change it all around
Did i break the frame

I want to know how did i rate
what did i mean
is this the way
Dirty Girls Get Clean?

Do i scrub up nice
is it worth the sacrifice

pg. 2

Nov 22

I just returned from the Village Recorder. Last night with Corgan. I love him so much. he takes good care of me. we wrote 7 songs and he was incredibly supportive. we recalibrated, reframed, and really got in deep.

I dont understand this concept of publishing my diaries although i didnt mind publishing has had become so fucking objectified I just stopped caring what people thought, now i do. i wish i could take it back. But I cant. and on and on Dirty blonde.

and on and on and on your dirty blonde

Dec 24th –

I'm awaiting some wedding from anthropologie. & bought Fez a bunch. and from Tiffany => i got he a key necklace and some beautiful rememb. diamonds: platinum. i so did am a little girl cld be very happy to see the Tiffany box because you mi just that beautiful Tiffany blue. i could paint a room Tiffany blue. i could find the town Tiffany blue.

anne sextons ironical sense that she was betteroff than the public who considered her crazy offers a a design for anyone like me.
I have to MAKE MY OWN WORLD instead of succumbing to the one that presses on me. I have to turn the tables on the lie wich tries to appear as fate & the full weight of the DA'S office against all odds must keep my wits about me and refuse to surrender to anyone or anything less than divine.
I must be faithful to the mystery taking place in my heart — rather than <u>ANY</u> system wich would try whatever the motive to disempower me. to own me. The strategy of Eccentricity

I felt kurt tonight when i was Chanting. all up in my heart. ~~[illegible]~~

~~Genuine Grief. Clean Grief. not mixed~~ In with anything. you know that guy was so sophisticated & witty. I know we'd still be together despite my doubts. he could hang. Justin that sort of Compatability Comes once In a

blue moon. I genuinely deeply miss him & wherever he is he knows it. it burns me up that im a "widow". i hate the word. and i hate hate what this has done to my beautiful daughter - hardened her edges even more than i have. her soft & blurry beautiful bumpy clumsy edges. oh Frances bean you are the Queen & your daddy was a prince i wish

Risk unmanaged why
Rock n roll nigger is the most superior
song in the canon of recorded rock n roll music.
as the JT leroy Hoax suggests Heterosexual
woman ~~cann~~ cannot make it on their own.
They must pretend to be something that
they are not. Even a nuetered transgendered
former Aids riddled street hustler ~~protected~~
by a network of gay mafia is preferable to
being a semi educated straight female. which is
a third the reason Rock n roll nigger
aspires to true religious greatness
a straight woman with no predecessor
no support system no paradigm grabbing
at imagery as though it were her last day
on earth. ~~the~~ socially appropriate. the usage of
the screech "nigger" is a blandishment in your face forever tattooed. I've watched over & over as people squirm at the lyrics of neighboring song)
Patti is making it socially appropriate & fuck
you very much if you dont agree or understand.
as old as this song gets it never fails
~~to~~ put me in a trance.

Its not about love......most of my songs are.
the ones that are not aspire to be cocky like
this. it cannot be topped. not for time,
there will never be 1979 ever again. not for
bravery. there will never be pre patti Smith.
pre hip hop. not for original thought. There will
never be an opportunity to dare people to
Think one a racist when one is so obviously
not. not for literacy. showing some of the
best poetic imagary into an incredibly nuanced
rock n roll song and pulling it off cannot be
done twice in a generation or five. There is
nothing to do with this song but stand back
in awe and know youve been hustled,
beaten, ass kicked and that you are in
witness to a true religious experience.
its risk. pure adrenline chemic risk.
There is zero refuge in this song.
no cock is coming out at the end to
comfort you with its stability and heterogenous
boringness. you are transported to a crotch
dampening wilderness of pre punk pre post punk
pre rock fanzine writer nonsense "ethos" spouting
nonsense. If you cant cry upon hearing this song then
do not count yourself among the wild hearted
young americans. Shine on. Shine on.

I read JT Leroy "Hair" piece
in the New Yorker in absolute horror
I feel like the ceiling fell in. what a
lame bitch. all those hours on the phone
with her, all that investment of my
time. all that breathless nonsense.
i went off JT 2-3 years ago. to the point
of allergen. a real chemic phobia
developed. neil asked me to write a
piece for a rock n roll book, but when
i saw JT had had a complete taste
lapse & devoted God knows 10,000 words
or something to Dave Grohl, i felt it was
such a disconnect that the meditation i
wanted to do on a sacrament of
rock music such as "Rock n Roll Nigger"
(Patti's) would be wasted. shallow
shoved that tasteless idiot — who cannot
BUY her credibility a new paradigm

You were beautiful
You were Glorious
now your all covered in loserdust
You were fabulous
You were Gorgeous
now your all covered in loserdust
all the things Im about
to crush
all the things i used to trust
your youth is gone, its turned to rust
its all covered in loserdust
na nana your going down for
Chachacha what you done — pray
your going down for your loser
dust

hey hey here she comes now
Everyone look while i knock him to the ground

Sit down
motherfucker
I'm gonna
have you now
Stand up motherfucker
against the wall ... I'm gonna let you down
Standup motherfucker
I'm gonna get you out
Sit down motherfucker all
I'm gonna take you ~~all~~ down

You come to me with your
ducks lined up, all up in a line
You had a plan all along
to take away all that was mine
You come to me in sorrow
& you come to me in disgrace
Come back here tomorrow
I'll wipe that smirk right off your face

You
Come to
me about
whose the coolest
person & the hottest
theres just one rule
you're broken baby
dont Ever rape
a Goddess

You come to me with tears in your eyes
& you come to me all wrong
You come to me with more lies
& all you getting baby is this song
You come in sorrow
& you come to me in disgrace
Come back here tomorrow
I'll wipe that smirk right off your face
You let them come & rape my life
You told me things you wouldn't tell your wife
You come to me with tabloids
& you come to me with sleaze
I'll wipe ~~that~~ her sparkle kiss off your lips
I'll have you on your knees
You come to me injectable
& powdered to ingest
I never was respectable, still
But at least i was dressed.
You come to me bloody but somehow untamed
I want total surrender
& I want it from you now
~~You come to me begging for one last time~~ more
~~I look into those rock n roll eyes~~
I've reversed anything mere resigned.
You've come to me in chaos & all your moves
are wrong. in the dead of night i never wanted anything more than you.
But all your getting is this song

they think were Evil dumb & lazy
oversexed loudmouthed & Crazy
They think wed marry them for money
if we Could
& the silly cunts among us really would
we are represented by the small
& the big among us fall
into chains and into maulings by our own
and they know this from the start
& it breaks just breaks my heart
they think that in the End it isnt
us that really rules the world
thats where they are deluded
because in this dark age precluded
as we are
from living proper lifes and being
forced to act like Girls and
being dragged & tortured into Confessing
on our Choking bleeding deathbeds that
ahem ahem it must be a mans world

they think were fools
they think were ninnies
and God forbid if
we arent skinny
and if i could id just be gay
id make them all just go away
and if i could id just castrate them
I swear to God i fucking hate them
as much as they hate me
they think were stupid swooning bitches
they think were 28 day bloody witches
they ~~want~~ to burn me at the stake
and put a knife right through my heart
and turn the weak of us against
the strong
and turn woman into girls
and make the worst of us into predators
its a bloody mans private world

I know the truth, call me a whore
but I'll just tell the truth some more
Take my money destroy my life
make it insane for me to ever be
anybody's wife
Tear me down again & again
make me so lonely i could die
without a friend
make me long for firearms
make me wimper for a noose
but by the crack of dawn
I'll be so drunk with the truth
Call me honey call me baby
call me your princess your little Girl
pull the diamonds from my holes
~~Make~~ me to long lost shores
exile
but yall never ~~catch~~ me snarling
that I'm lost in a mans world
& I'll never equate all that I am
with who I fuck with who I reflect
with who I am as a man.
Fuck off.

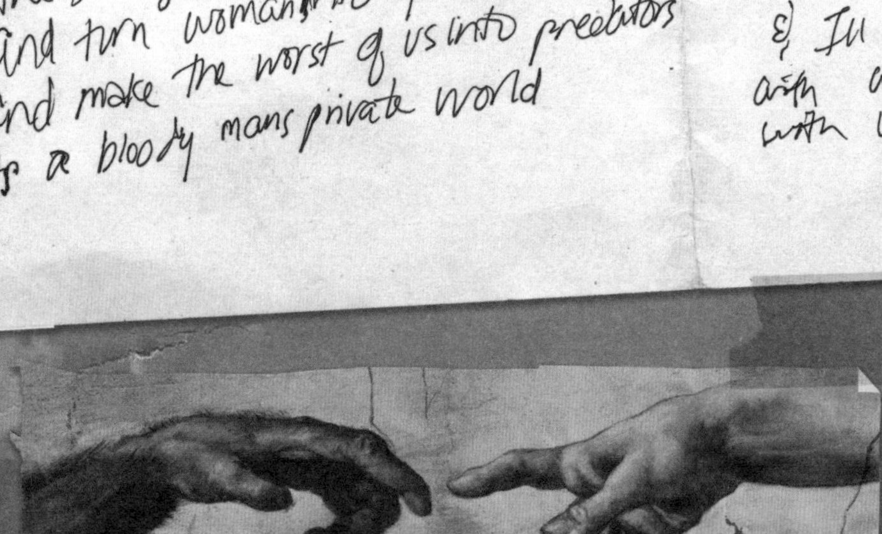

the depths of my despair

& it isnt fair
the depths of my despair
I cant take it anymore
when I get it wrong, i really get it wrong
and it lasts forever OK
I am stuck with you
no Rewards no proof
I cant take you anymore

& it isnt fair
the depths of my despair
I have a right to be this wrong
if theres hope its fading
all of me is aching
If theres life in this its gone

& it cant be real
how sick & dark this feels
how its a mistake that im alive
I can drink and drink
to blot out my think
have another one or five

~~I~~ was born ~~Innocent~~ too
take my toys back I can't share
but come a little closer
see
the depths of my
despair

take me down a peg or two
Spill my secrets don't you dare
face to face with the
abyss known
as the
depths of my
despair

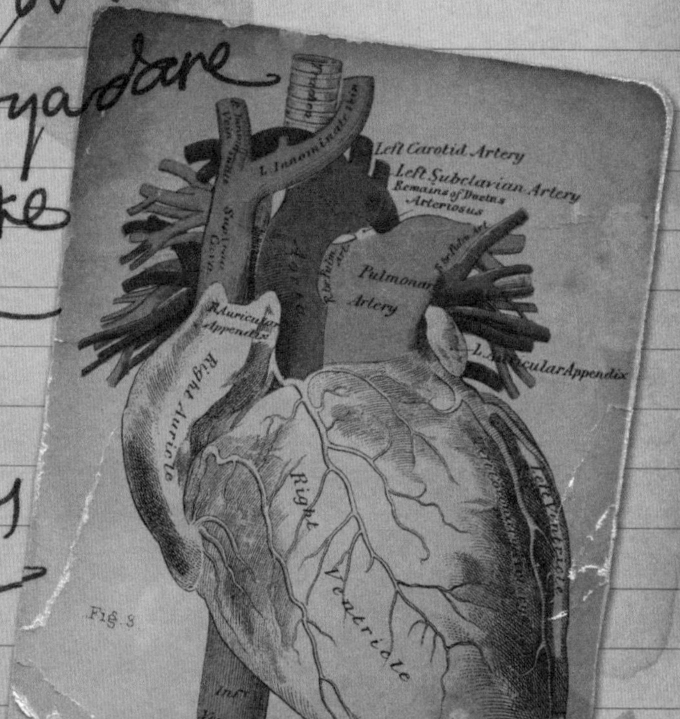

Like a broken diamond
Like a keening nightmare
you're the only game
in town (one who knows)
the depths of my despair

broken babydoll

~~Like~~ a
waking up from a nightmare
I need just some relief
from the depths of my despair

I told you simply everything
took it all off I laid bare
now you Lord it for all to see
the depths of my despair

~~Your welcome to it~~
Your welcome to it

----------Original Message----------

From: [Courtney Love]

To: [Lindsay Lohan]

Subject: keep your chin up

Date: Sat, 07 Jan 2006 21:35:03

I was at the gym today and you should know that noone really gives a hoot about this woman trying to make a name for herself. I was thinking about you and looked around and we were all just ignoring the nonsense ...I remember reading my first VF - my cover was nicer but the first article was a fucking nightmare - I thought the world had split open and was going to swallow me whol.e and all i wanted to do was kill that woman...I realise now that as hardcore as it was , it made me alot more interesting and somehow employable. Keep your chin up. Noones giving it a second thought. I bet its hard because your in it, but just keeo creative and surrounded by good people. Courtney

[Lindsay Lohan]

To: Court L

Subject: Re: keep your chin up

Date: Sun, 8 Jan 2006 05:22:34 +0000 GMT

You first off, are so amazing, and introspective and kind and I really admire your perspective on things, as well you taking the time to be so curteous in my situation and these sickofans that invest in our lives that we work hard for and aspire to have. People that are so unhappy with their own lives they have to pry and lie about anothers...

But again, you, second off, its really rad that you're even emailing me and have so much care to give me your insight because you're bloody fucking genius in all the things you do, amongst all the shit you've been through...

Can we meet sometime and talk and chat like normal people so that I can pick your brain?

... Also, my mommy says hello and she loves you tons. Hehe :) ... I need to go to a gym!!! Peace and love. . Til soon xxL

my mommy is a very very good
mommy. Vomit.
I hope she Enjoyed her nick Broomfield
15 minutes. it was more like Four.
I knew she'd do it someday.
and just like her, she bet
against me. She bet wrong.

April 17th
2006

I went to Liz Taylors Easter Egg
party yesterday & i was summoned by dame
Elizabeth to her bathroom where she
put her goddess hands on my head weighed
down with the diamond "Krupp" : "Burton-Taylor"
Burton had given her (upon asking how she got it
she replied "I was bored darling") & said
to her little retinue "we love sweet
Courtney dont we" in that voice

you know its over
it just has to be
your the worst thing that ever happened to me
your the only thing I really want

if there anyplace that you de…
Early in the morning
after a dark night of the sou…
you cannot keep a secret
Im too young to feel this old

my dirty little secret has
a dirty little name
never felt so used
never felt ~~so lame~~ such shame
Hell hath nothing like the day i was born
I'll be what you want
Gods own sweet porn
Hell hath no fury
like the mess I'll make
like the heads will roll
like the names I'll take.

down dim down
past beyond all sex
where you drag me yeah
Im delirious
I stumble there trying to Escape
but even I cannot prevent my own rape

my house is so outrageously beautiful & crazy sexy
& my ballroom is covered in cherry blossoms
& lilacs & its fabulous. & really really lonely.
I work at the most beautiful studio in
CA & come home to the most beautiful house
I've ever seen. I feel so fucking blessed.
& to have Linda - who's the hottest songwriter
& producer on this planet & Billy who is such
a complete melodic genius both. working at 100%
on this I just feel so lucky. & I'm not
paying anything everyone's doing everything for free.
are the bad stuff just seems to have fucking
evaporated - as long as i walk this Road &
have nothing to hide.

This Record is going into a magical magestic
place. the shabby demos aren't even
skeletons at this point. its dreamy & sexy &
magical & beautiful & dark. it doesn't compromise
who I am in the least. Billy played guitar
in New Order as a study in humility &
they Gifted him with Ian's vocal effects box
& the ~~joy~~ division amp & head. We've
come up with an arrangement for "Love Will Tear Us
Apart" that is as good if not better than the
original or obviously I wouldn't touch it. &
Peter (Hook) is I hear going to play bass on it.

My heart is a tabloid
& Im guilty as sin
~~I swear youre~~

your a very bad boy
and you just pull me
back In

They dont value sweet
or dignity or death
& theyre ~~treacling~~ bilesleeze with their ~~gutter~~
~~will hand my last breath~~ bile breath
but baby I just melt like a butterpot
I have so much to say
but theres no saying that
X it is what it is
X and its not enough

I've got a use for you
I'm not through with you
I've got a noose for you
I've got news for you
I'll tell you when this is through
4 you

you ~~play~~ fuck so dirty
& you ~~play~~ fuck too rough
& why can't i seduce ~~you~~ everyone else
they look at me
& they can just can tell
Im ice cream all melted
just a puddle on the floor
Im bruised & Im whelted
& I feel like a whore.
go and clean up your mess bitch
you left my Guts on the floor
and i've had enough of you
but I cant find the door

my heart is a tabloid
its been left to exploit
Im guilty as sin
But Id do it all over again

Im guilty as sin
& In no time Id do it again
my heart is a tabloid
Whats left of it is null & void
But Fire rain & death cannot stop me
from trying
until theres nothing left
but a ghost and she ~~that is~~ crying
Coz this is the day oh when youre gone
this is the day you walk alone

its never - enough got burnt when
you can look at him but you cant touch
hes ~~at~~ always trouble in the Rubble
been left here
But wind fire & speed cannot stop my climb
& dark Raging waves will not hide your
Crime ~~Coz this is the~~.

I knew a man who came from the clouds
who was the only one to ever say those
things out loud.
I knew a boy who came from the sea
who was the only boy who ever knew the truth about me

I saw a demon sometime around dawn
& my dirty little secret lies in your heart its all wrong

I knew a ~~myth~~ boy who fell from the sky
he chewed me up & spit me out

Im overwrought & undersexed
baby what did you expect
Im underwhelmed & so disgraced
I cant even hide to save my face
these hypocrites & succubus
theyll never understand us
your toadies live in the underbelly
where noone says anything sweet about me

never have
I sunk so low
Im shipwrecked
& only you know
how to cure my
fevered brow
baby what did
you to do me now
~~[illegible]~~
its a nightmare
of fever dreams —

the rose parade came to town
~~& when it left~~, ~~it left me naked~~, it left me
made me a princess stole my crown
I knew a ~~demon~~ angel who came
from the fog
and now im got the gods Im calling on
Im lonely & totally bored
I dont know what to do with my hands now
I surrender, I give in
Ill kick down your door just let me in

have I burnt down
all my bridges
have I burnt down all
my walls
Is there anyone still standing for me
can you hear me
anyone at all.

if i ever kissed & told
baby wed all be lost
but i will never kiss & tell
and look oh look at what it cost

& you know
Im drowning
& you know
Im drowning
Your whole world is in
my hands.
Your whole wide world is in
my hands.

& Ive lost myself completely

I look to you my shooting star
Im on the pacific coast highway
my God how did you fall so far!

I knew a boy who felt like a doll
he was only 24 inches full length tall

open my throat
make it a slash
do the tabloids pay your case
I'm in danger of exploding
my whole world is just imploding

and i crush what i love the most
but for the love of a
broken man & a ~~broken~~ stubborn ghost

~~How~~ bad do you want it yeah
How badly do you need it bitch
Every baby needs a daddy
even if its just a little bit
& you feed me lines all night
they taste real good, sparkling lies
would you pick me so apart
would you ravage my black heart
tearing me from limb to limb
tell me to begin again —

Hell hath no fury
like the day i was born
block out my email
go back to your porn
& when your shivering & naked
& theres noone left
when your just about to take
your very last breath
remember that you are guilty as sin
you've got none but yourself
to blame for the shit you are in
you gave yourself time to me
time to turn yourself in

It does not end until I decide
always the bridesmaid never the bride
Im colder than you
Im harder than you
& I will see this all the way through

pg.

Dear Kurt:

please put a hex on Frannies teacher.
he called, and after 6 years at this
school our perfect daughter has a
behavioral problem: shes too popular.
She humiliated her in front of her class
by calling her the "Queen Bee"
he told me that shes most popular –
and you'll be pleased – shes nice to the oddballs
& misfits shes "mean" to the aspirants
he said shes a little "drunk with her own power!"
he said there are kids whose day rises & falls
upon whether Frances says hello to them. see
Drunk with power? me. Imperious & random? you
Key chic word noone knows of yet?. "Rare"
he said the little girls were going to
(imagine...) rise up against her. then he started
in on how "I know you Courtney Love" nonsense
In any case shes officially branded and now
... wants him fired. (I think thats [illegible])
please come home. I dont think you'd like
the man I love. but he reminds me
of you. Love
your wife

& your ghost it shudders through me
I'm covered in diamonds & filth
but that wich destroys me
merely covers up my guilt.

& i'll never see the end of this
like a phantom i expect
& ive lost the heart of everything
Ive lost my self repect

& my hands are blackly scarlet
they are all covered in blood
from all the damage ive done
to those that i have loved

Sunday
i believe ive got a cure for ya all
Sunday
will ya be there after it all.

Drowning horses tangled up in black knots Slap me so much harder
that can't be all you've got.

Lovely get off of the ride!
but ive been dead for years and years
alive when you
Then see you on the other side

the angel in you
is the danger in me
theyve managed you
that theres none to believe
the thing that you did
made everyone [illegible] alive
at there before god
the ghost of you
is the ghost in me
all that wretched integrity
where ever ever gonna [illegible]
where is it now?
what is the point?
all the damage you've done
like a god they commit
& the horses are drowning
in the gutter & the streets
& nooses coming
you —
and no this isn't a dream

At least i know
theres some hope
& Im not ashamed
of where Ive been
but I never want
to go ^there^ again
& my wigs on crooked
& I got no shoes
& ~~I sit and~~ rock back & forth
& ~~I~~ wait for you
a shred of dignity
not too much sorrow
a ~~little~~ bit of hope
hold out for tomorrow
crimes crush your spirit
& you wonder ~~God~~ can you hear us
~~tell~~ ~~go~~ survive this mess i made
are you my salvation babe?
& when its black
& its a hole
& its poison
no room for a soul
absence of light
has come to your door
nothing ~~but~~ but miles and miles &
sorrow

Its a long drive back where
we started from
All the trouble weve seen
all the lies weve told
Its early in the morning after a
~~black~~ night of the soul
dont you feel like i do?
too young to feel this old?
when you start to undress in this
long black limousine
I get this taste in my mouth
Its ~~all some~~
~~what~~ Ive already seen
& If i could only have one hit of you
a blast a hint a taste a clue
when you roll me all around
in that long black limousine
I see the sunset go down
on the sea on me obscene
& Im rushing all in bits coz now gone
hit a vein
I like ~~when~~ it hurts like this
take some pleasure from my pain

I was looking up at you
from the bottoms of my life
I was looking far to deep
and I started to go blind
I dont mortgage, I just rent
I look at you,
I'm not gonna get this get right
I'm just gonna repent
its early in the morning after
a long night of the soul
i get so tired of learning him
im too young to feel this old

i swear your killing me
it isnt fair the depths of my despair

on the radio
give it to me as hard as you got

like a million
obstacles
I dont know if id dare
to part the seas
& face it down
the depths of my
despair

how can i possibly repent
when i dont mortgage i just rent
Ill never get you right
Someone made an expose
about a thing id never betray
You'll never see the light

Happy Ending Story

Hey I burn better in the dark
dont let the light in
its pure poison where ya are
Is that me crying

Hey for every ending tragedy
hey I'll ~~smash~~ ~~that dust in~~
~~tear~~ your heart out
for-every evil dumb lazy
hey ill tear the sun down

Hey the Quicksands coming bitter end
Hey its that me crying
Hey the stars fall down dont let them in
hey is that me dying

~~Oh i swear your killing me, killing me~~
Hey the lights coming let it in
in all its glory
If its all bloody its a sin
come tell me ur story

Dear God
Its so lonely here
& im living on fear
Ive always been weird
and Ive always been scared
And now I am bitter
If your really there
Show me as Im scared,
why dont I fit in,
Always hustled my wits
my hips & my lips
theres got to be
something else
I feel the spirit
so strong
but you got me
so wrong
how am I
so flawed

Dear God
how am I so flawed.
Did you really mess up
Was I just a mistake?
Come on just fess up.

I'm looking for my other half
two cripples they can walk
All the shiny things Im shown
that i can never have
That i dont do
but i sure talk
and im buried to you in trance
and i havent got a prayer
If you ~~are~~ exist take a chance
I wont tell anyone your there.

Give me your arms filled with my
sorrow
Give me your soul overflowing with grief
Give it to me now i will not
wait for tomorrow

Give me back what you stole you thief

This is the end
of my Journal
like it or not

AFTERWORD:

TAKE THE CAKE, GIRLS

COURTNEY LOVE IS already more exposed than her journals could possibly reveal. Still, you get the feeling that she'd be furious if she caught you reading her diaries. That is part of the essence of Courtney: contradiction. Hiding behind her dramatic persona is actually a very ordinary girl, a girl who seeks what *Valley of the Dolls* author Jacqueline Susann called "mass love" and yet doesn't edit herself for the sake of public approval. She's one of those rare people who might be exactly the same wherever she is and whomever she is with, whether she is walking down the red carpet or alone in her house checking her e-mail. She's always Courtney Love, difficult but rewarding.

In many ways *Dirty Blonde* is a kind of performance, just like her Hole shows, her star turns as Althea Leasure (Larry Flynt's wife) or Lynn Margulies (Andy Kaufman's girlfriend), and her make-outs with Drew Barrymore. She's bad and brilliant, surprising and predictable. Performing comes naturally to Courtney, as do her other notable attributes: being passionate, political, spontaneous, and vicious. Despite Courtney's sporadic claims that she doesn't want these pages published—she loves to be in the public eye.

But why does the public care about Courtney Love? Why should her diaries be published? People love Courtney in part because she is easy to hate—fulfilling the role of "bad" woman and embodying all of our free-floating cultural anxieties about women in general. For some, she is a modern-day Yoko Ono—the real reason the guitar gods are no longer with us—and punished with rumors and anti-woman screeds. For others, she is simply iconic. She takes up space and causes problems and never says sorry. She is the spiritual daughter of Janis Joplin—wild, smart, sexy, boy-crazy, and vulnerable to the dark allure of drugs. She's a rawer version of Madonna: she isn't a victim of sex, she wields the power, and she controls her image. And yet, after all that, she's just an average girl we can all relate to: "In her little-girl dresses and bright red lipstick, Courtney Love gave more the impression of a child playing dress-up than of an adult rock star," writes Debbie Stoller, *Bust*'s cofounder and the coeditor of *The Bust Guide to the New Girl Order*. "Her girlie-girl style, coupled with her very unladylike, out-of-control performances, helped to convey her rebellion against the stereotype of the demure, selfless female and won her a loyal following of young women who were grasping for a model of female adulthood and sexuality that could include anger and aggression."

An amalgam of letters, e-mails, song lyrics, photos, and mementos, these diaries are the emotional fragments of an outcast girl, a troubled teenager, a striving twentysomething, a superstar mother, and a somewhat tragic figure. In response to that characterization, Courtney might say, *Fuck you*. Her ambition and her ability to constantly reinvent herself defy feminine conventions. She is unscripted—and that is a frightening state for a woman, which makes her all the more heroic.

People love Courtney because she's fragile and yet protects herself by being overconfident and by exposing herself before others get the satisfaction of doing so, not unlike other iconic (and tragic) women such as Marilyn Monroe and Billie Holiday. The fact is that Love is seeking attention for reasons many women understand—she wants love and feels ugly and drinks too much and makes mistakes, and all of this is part of her allure. She's not perfect, but she's powerful. She's human.

People care about Courtney because she is an icon—not due to her crazy antics, but because she has been an emboldening presence in the lives of so many women and girls. The real essence of Courtney is her impact, the storms she leaves in her wake, the gumption and defiance she so naturally inhabits and makes possible for others to possess. Because of Courtney Love, twenty-two-year-old women pick up guitars, sixteen-year-old girls in Ohio learn about feminism by coming across the word in a *SPIN* interview with Courtney, and in general women don't feel held back by society's expectation of what it means to be a lady. Girls and women, including us, have been inspired to be more aggressive and to ask for more because of Love's example.

"I want to be the girl with the most cake," she sings in "Doll Parts." And who wouldn't want to be?

—JENNIFER BAUMGARDNER AND AMY RICHARDS

NEW YORK CITY • JUNE 2006

NOTES and CHRONOLOGY

Unless otherwise noted, all letters represent drafts of correspondence.

PAGE 4
Drawing, 1972.

PAGE 5
At top: Gateway Montessori School, San Francisco. Courtney (three years old), bottom row, second from left. California, 1968. At bottom: Marcola, Oregon, with her sister Nicole. Photograph by F. Rodriguez, 1972.

PAGE 9
Excerpt from letter, written while Courtney was attending an all-girls' private boarding school in New Zealand, 1976.

PAGE 10
School photo, fourth grade, Oregon, ca. 1973.

PAGES 11–13
In March of 1976, Courtney auditioned for the Mickey Mouse Club and received this rejection. At the time she went by the nickname "Coco" and used her adoptive stepfather's last name. The writing at the bottom of pages 11–13 is ca. 2002.

PAGES 14–15
Bay City Rollers collage by Courtney, ca. 1976.

PAGES 16–17
Excerpt from a letter written to her stepfather while at Skipworth Juvenile Detention Center in Eugene, Oregon, March 1978. Courtney was sent to Skipworth after being convicted of shoplifting, and remained at the facility for approximately one year.

PAGES 18–31
Diary entries and poems written at the Hillcrest School of Oregon, where Courtney was a ward of the state, from 1978 to 1980. Hillcrest is a correctional lockdown facility for girls.

PAGE 32
Diary entry, Dublin, 1981.

PAGE 33
Japan, summer 1981. Courtney and friend.

PAGES 34–45
Diary entries, Liverpool, 1982.

PAGE 34
Postcard in journal, Liverpool.

PAGE 35
Photograph of Courtney in Sefton Park, Liverpool, 1982, by Robin Barbur, a friend from Portland, Oregon, who joined Courtney during her stay in the U.K. List of top records: "Roxy" = Roxy Music; *Young Americans*, David Bowie; *Stage*, David Bowie; *Heaven Up Here*, Echo & The Bunnymen; *Marquee Moon*, Television; Siouxsie and the Banshees; Patti Smith; "P.I.L." = Public Image Limited; Faust (early 1970s German rock band); "J.D's" = Joy Division; "E.B." = Echo & The Bunnymen; "Cope" = Julian Cope (founding member and front man of the Teardrop Explodes). Liverpool, 1982.

PAGE 36
"Scouse" = Scouser, British slang for a native or resident of Liverpool; "Scallie" = scallywag; "Council Estate" = British government housing.

PAGE 37
Letter to Linda Carroll, Courtney's mother, Liverpool, 1982.

PAGES 38–39
Overlay: excerpt from poem. "Eric's" = legendary Liverpool punk club; "F. Scott" = F. Scott Fitzgerald; "Baudelaire" = Charles Baudelaire.

PAGE 41
"Mac" = Ian McCulloch; "Tom Verlaine" = front man of the band Television; "Julie" = Julian Cope; "Deb Iyall" = front woman of the band Romeo Void; "Ju" = Julian Cope. Photograph by F. Rodriguez, Portland, Oregon, 1981.

PAGE 42
Postcard in journal, London, 1982. Song list, Liverpool, 1982.

PAGE 43
"Mac" = Ian McCulloch (front man of Echo & The Bunnymen); "Ju" = Julian Cope; "EBM" = Echo & The Bunnymen. On left: Julian Cope; on right: Robin Barbur.

PAGE 45
Goodbye to Liverpool, diary entry, Heathrow Airport, 1982.

PAGES 46–49
Span 1982–84.

PAGE 49
"Roddy Frame" = songwriter, singer, guitarist of Aztec Camera; "Richard Butler" = lead singer of the Psychedelic Furs and later Love Spit Love.

PAGE 50
Diary cover, ca. 1984.

PAGE 51
Photograph of French poet Arthur Rimbaud. "Johnny Marr" = guitarist and founder, with singer Morrissey, of The Smiths. Paris, France, ca. 1984.

PAGES 52–66
San Francisco, 1985.

PAGES 54–55
"Keats" = British poet John Keats; "Funkadelic" = band; "Aidan Quinn" = actor; "Judd Nelson" = actor; "Her lost Kat" = Kat Bjelland, roommate and bandmate (guitarist) in Sugar Baby Doll aka Sugar Babylon; "My Micheal" = Michael "Mooneye" Mooney, Liverpool scenester, guitarist for Psychedelic Furs, Julian Cope, Spiritualised, and Lupine Howl; "Gloria Swanson" = actress.

PAGE 58
"Roddy" = Roddy Bottum, keyboard player for Faith No More. San Francisco, 1985. Courtney with Kat Bjelland at the 1993 Lollapalooza Festival, at which Babes in Toyland was headlining. Photograph by Jeffrey Thurnher.

PAGES 62–63
"Quiet Room" song lyrics inspired by Hillcrest School of Oregon during the Sugar Baby Doll aka Sugar Babylon period. "Byrons" = Lord Byron; "Caroll Baker" = Carroll Baker, actress and star of the 1956 film *Baby Doll*, written by Tennessee Williams and directed by Elia Kazan; "Lawrence Olivier" = Laurence Olivier, British actor; "Vivien" = Vivien Leigh, British actress. San Francisco, 1985. An early Sugar Baby Doll aka Sugar Babylon band photo, Courtney and Kat Bjelland appear on the left. Courtney's character study for the part of Nancy Spungen in the movie *Sid and Nancy: Love Kills*, directed by Alex Cox.

PAGE 64
"Best Sunday Dress," lyrics from Sugar Baby Doll aka Sugar Babylon song; Courtney would later perform the song with Hole.

PAGE 65
In August of 1985, Courtney traveled to Los Angeles for her audition as Nancy Spungen in *Love Kills*. Though the part would go to Chloe Webb, Courtney was cast as Nancy's friend Gretchen. "Jennifer Finch" = friend and bassist for Sugar Baby Doll aka Sugar Babylon. To-do list for acting career: "LK" = *Sid and Nancy: Love Kills*. San Francisco, 1985.

PAGE 66
After working with Courtney on *Love Kills*, Alex Cox would cast her in the role of Velma, one of the lead characters in his next film *Straight to Hell*, which also starred Joe Strummer. Written in London, ca. 1986.

PAGES 67–68
London, ca. 1986.

PAGE 68
"Fall" = The Fall, seminal British indie/post-punk band; "John Taylor" = bassist in Duran Duran.

PAGE 69
Bullet-point biography of Jean Harlow. *Hell's Angels* refers to the 1930 film starring Harlow and directed by Howard Hughes. Courtney would portray Harlow in an off-Broadway production called *The Beard*. New York City, ca. 1987.

PAGE 70
Courtney as Velma in Alex Cox's film *Straight to Hell*. Photograph by Tom Collins, 1987.

PAGE 71
Résumé, ca. 1987.

PAGES 72–78
New York City, ca. 1987.

PAGE 72
"Genet" = Jean Genet, French novelist and playwright.

PAGE 74
"Blake" = friend.

PAGES 79–82
London, 1987.

PAGE 79
Refers to the London premiere of *Straight to Hell*; "The Columbia" = infamous London hotel favored by musicians; "Harlows" = Jean Harlow.

PAGE 81
"Gabby" = Joe Strummer's girlfriend; "Mick" = Mick Jones of The Clash and Big Audio Dynamite (B.A.D.).

PAGE 83
Front cover of a diary written in Minneapolis, Minnesota, 1987–88.

PAGES 84–87
Minneapolis, 1987–88.

PAGE 85
"Cricket" = Courtney.

PAGE 90
"Sweet Crystal Powered by God" = idea for band name, Minneapolis, Minnesota, 1989; "Dicknail Clouds" = Dicknail b/w Clouds 7-inch single released on Sub Pop in March 1991, ca. 1990.

PAGES 92–93
"John Peel" = influential British disc jockey, ca. 1990.

PAGES 94–95
Los Angeles, ca. 1990.

PAGES 96–97, 99–102, 104, 108, 117
Hole show flyers by Courtney, Los Angeles, 1992.

PAGE 105
Letter to Thurston Moore of Sonic Youth, 1990.

PAGE 106
"K" = Kat Bjelland, Los Angeles, 1990.

PAGE 107
Hole publicity photograph by Michael Lavine featuring the original lineup: (*left to right*) Courtney, Caroline Rue (drummer), Eric Erlandson, and Jill Emery (bassist).

PAGE 109
Draft of track order for *Pretty on the Inside*, debut Hole LP, Los Angeles, 1990.

PAGES 110–11
Los Angeles, 1991.

PAGE 112
Letter to Kim Gordon of Sonic Youth, who along with Don Fleming would coproduce *Pretty on the Inside*. Courtney and Kim are pictured here at England's annual Reading Festival, in 1991.

PAGE 113
Los Angeles, 1991.

PAGE 114
Photograph by Juergen Teller.

PAGE 115
"Mrs. Jones," song from *Pretty on the Inside*. Los Angeles, 1991.

PAGE 116
"Pussy Galore" = American noise-rock band that formed in Washington, D.C., in 1985. Los Angeles, 1991; "Eric" = Eric Erlandson, guitarist and founding member of Hole.

PAGE 117
Lyrics, 1991; "T-Rex" = British band led by guitarist and front man Marc Bolan; "Wipers" = The Wipers, a Portland, Oregon, band.

PAGE 118
Draft of liner notes for *Pretty on the Inside*: "Kate Belljar" = Kat Bjelland, front woman of Babes in Toyland; "Long Gone John" = founder of the indie record label Sympathy for the Record Industry; "Joe Cole" = close friend of Courtney's and roadie for Hole, was shot and killed in the company of his close friend author/musician Henry Rollins, during a robbery at Rollins's home, December 19, 1991; "Sister Finch" = Jennifer Finch, bassist in Sugar Baby Doll aka Sugar Babylon, ca. 1997, and bassist of L7; "Roddy B. / RC Bottum" = keyboard player in Faith No More; "Rob Graves / Rob Ritter" = bass player in legendary Los Angeles punk rock bands The Bags, Gun Club, and 45 Grave, died of heroin overdose in 1991; "Al Flipside" = editor of *Flipside Fanzine*, which later became *Flipside Magazine*; "Sub Pop Records" = Seattle, Washington, indie record label, which first signed among others Nirvana, Soundgarden, and Mudhoney. Diary entry, Los Angeles, 1991.

PAGE 119
Hole promotional photograph by Steve Gullick. Patty Schemel (drums), Kristen Pfaff (bass; died of an overdose in June 1994), Eric Erlandson, and Courtney, 1993.

PAGES 120–27
1991.

PAGES 124–25
"Sick Stealer Friend" = Kat Bjelland; "Her band" = Babes in Toyland; "Calamity Jane" = band; "Leadbelly" = folk singer; "N.W." = Pacific Northwest. 1991.

PAGE 126
"This Record" = *Pretty on the Inside*, 1991.

PAGE 129
Courtney leaning out of Babes in Toyland tour bus, Lollapalooza, photograph by Jeffrey Thurnher, 1993. Diary entry, ca. 1991.

PAGES 130–31
Courtney, photograph by Steve Gullick.

PAGE 132
"S.B." = Santa Barbara, California; "Mudhoney" = band; "Mark" = Mark Arm, singer for Mudhoney; "Janet" = Janet Billig, Courtney's on-and-off-again manager between ca. 1990 and 2003, 1991. Photograph of Courtney and Kurt, 1992.

PAGES 134–35
Fax to Kurt Cobain from Courtney, December 1991; Kurt, photograph by Courtney, 1992. Letters to Kurt from Courtney, 1992.

PAGES 136–43
"And She's Not Even Pretty" = fanzine created by Courtney in 1992.

PAGE 139
" 'St' Francis" = Frances Farmer, actress.

PAGES 140–41
"Pisces" = Rob Ritter, musician and friend; "Aries" = Joe Cole, roadie, tour manager, Henry Rollins's best friend, murdered in 1991. Bottom right: wedding photo, Waikiki Beach, February 24, 1992.

PAGE 143
Bottom left: Kim Deal of The Breeders.

PAGE 144
Bottom: art on final page of *And She's Not Even Pretty*.

PAGE 145
Hole, photograph by Steve Gullick. Left: Jill Emery, bass; right: Courtney. 1991.

PAGE 146
Kurt, photograph by Courtney, 1992.

PAGE 148
Contact sheet for *Sassy* magazine cover photo shoot by Michael Lavine, 1992.

PAGES 150–52
Ca. 1992.

PAGE 151
Photograph of Kurt with Frances Bean taken by Courtney, 1992. Photograph of Kurt waving taken while visiting with author William S. Burroughs, in Lawrence, Kansas, 1993.

PAGE 153
Kurt, Dylan Carlson (a musician and Kurt's best friend), and Mark Lanergan (lead singer and guitarist of Screaming Trees) in drag. Photographs by Courtney, 1992. Letter to Chrissie Hynde of the Pretenders, ca. 1992.

PAGE 154
Kurt and Frances Bean Cobain, photograph by Courtney, 1992.

PAGE 155
Courtney and Frances Bean, photograph by Guzman, 1992.

PAGE 156
Photograph of Kurt by Guzman, 1992.

PAGE 157
Kurt's baby picture, taken ca. 1967, with Courtney's writing on the back.

PAGES 158–59
Photograph of Frances Bean, marked up by Kurt. Courtney and Francis Bean, photograph by Stephen Sweet, ca. 1992. "NOV 93": despite the date that appears here, the year is actually 1992. Photograph of Kurt and Courtney by Dora Handel. Family snapshot, Christmas 1992.

PAGES 160–61
Lyrics, ca. 1993. Photograph of Courtney by Michel Comte. Courtney and Kurt at a benefit for Rock Against Rape, at Hollywood's Club Lingerie, the only time they ever played together in public, photograph by Lisa Johnson, 1993.

PAGES 162–63
Ca. 1992.

PAGE 164
Courtney, photograph by Kurt, 1992.

PAGE 166
Courtney, photograph by Jeffrey Thurnher.

PAGE 167
"Darby Crash" = singer for the band the Germs; "Robert Zimmerman" = Bob Dylan; "Perry Farrell" = singer for the band Jane's Addiction; "Lenny Bruce" = comedian; "Karl Lagerfeld" = designer; "Grace Kelly" = actress; "Anne Sexton" = writer, poet.

PAGE 168
Seattle, Washington, ca. 1994; the heart-shaped box sent to Kurt by Courtney, and for which the Nirvana song would later be named.

PAGE 170
Photographs by Guzman, 1992.

PAGE 171
Family photographs by Courtney.

PAGE 172
Childhood pictures of Kurt: (*top and bottom right*) Kurt's eighth birthday, February 20, 1975; (*bottom left*) Kurt, one year and ten months; (*top left*) Kurt, age one.

PAGE 174
From a letter to Billy Corgan of the Smashing Pumpkins. "Lanegan, Dylan" = Mark Lanegan of the Screaming Trees and Dylan Carlson, Kurt's best friend; "Michael S." = Michael Stipe, singer and front man of the band R.E.M.; "crush w/eyeliner" = R.E.M. song of the same name and written about Courtney. Photo: (*left to right*) Michael Stipe, Courtney, and actor Stephen Dorff after an R.E.M. concert. Tokyo, 1995.

PAGE 175
Courtney, photograph by Mark Seliger, late April 1994.

PAGE 176
"Doll Parts" video shoot by Samuel Bayer, 1995.

PAGES 178–79
Hole, photographs by Mark Seliger.

PAGE 180
Hole with Frances, photograph by Mark Seliger, ca. 1995. From left to right: Melissa Auf Der Maur, Eric Erlandson, Patty Schemel (standing), Courtney, and Frances.

PAGE 181
Hole, shot for their *Saturday Night Live* appearance, photographs by Edie Baskin, 1994; from left to right: Melissa, Patty, Courtney, and Eric.

PAGE 183
Courtney, photograph by Anton Corbijn, ca. 1995.

PAGE 184
Frances, photograph by Herb Ritts, ca. 1995.

PAGE 185
Snapshot of Courtney on the set of the movie *Beat*. Los Angeles, ca. 1997.

PAGE 186
Hawaii, 1996.

PAGE 187
Photograph by Stephane Sednaoui, 1997.

PAGE 188
Photograph of Elton John's fiftieth birthday party at Château Marmont. From left to right: Donatella Versace, Courtney, Elton John, and Elizabeth Taylor. March 1997.

PAGE 189
Pictured: Pete de Freitas, drummer for Echo & The Bunnymen, who died in a motorcycle accident in 1989.

PAGE 191
Courtney with Eric Erlandson during the recording of *Celebrity Skin*. Photograph by Kevin Westenberg, ca. 1998.

PAGE 192
Photographs by Steve Granitz and Carmen Valdes.

PAGE 194
Photograph by Rankin.

PAGE 195
Courtney, *SPIN* magazine, May 1994, photograph by Michel Comte.

PAGES 198–99
Courtney, photograph by Ellen Von Unwerth.

PAGES 200–201
Courtney as Althea Leasure in *The People vs. Larry Flynt*, 1996. Courtney and Kevyn Aucoin, photograph by Keith Milton for *Interview* magazine, 1997.

PAGE 204
Frances on her seventh birthday, photograph by Edward Norton, 1999.

PAGE 205
Courtney and Frances, Venice, ca. 1999.

PAGES 208–209
Dream, ca. 1999. Courtney and butterflies photograph by Ellen Von Unwerth.

PAGES 212–13
Courtney, photograph by Bruce Weber.

PAGE 214
Note from Marc Jacobs. "Beautiful gift" refers to a sweater of Kurt's she sent the designer.

PAGE 215
Photograph by Richard Avedon, New York, 1997.

PAGE 217
Photograph of Courtney by Jean-Baptiste Mondino.

PAGES 220–21
South of France, photograph by Jean-Baptiste Mondino during the recording of *America's Sweetheart*, May 2003.

PAGE 222
Photograph by Ian Hodgson.

PAGE 223
Photograph of Courtney with Hillary Clinton, taken at producer Lawrence Bender's fund-raising party for Clinton's senatorial campaign, September 28, 2000; additional drawing on photograph by Courtney.

PAGES 224–25
Essay by Courtney, "Gun Club for Girls," ca. 1999.

PAGE 227
Photograph by Steve Meisel.

PAGES 230–31
Sketches for an unrealized series of guitars for Fender to be called the Vista Venus, ca. 2003.

PAGE 233
Top left: Photograph by Jean-Baptiste Mondino, May 2003. Top right: Courtney performing with Elton John at a British charity concert. Bottom: Courtney with Milos Forman on the set of *Man on the Moon*. Photograph by François Duhamel, 1999.

PAGE 235
From *America's Sweetheart* photo shoot, photograph by David LaChapelle, ca. 2004.

PAGE 236
Richard Branson and Courtney, one day after she was arrested on Virgin Airlines, 2003.

PAGE 239
Frances, photograph by Jean-Baptiste Mondino, May 2003.

PAGE 240
Photograph by Ellen Von Unwerth, ca. 1998.

PAGES 242–43, 246–47
"How Dirty Girls Get Clean" lyrics, 2005.

PAGES 244–45
Photograph by Jean-Baptiste Mondino, May 2003.

PAGE 248
Bottom left: With Milos Forman at the ACLU ceremony in Forman's honor, 1997. Bottom right: Getting ready for the Oscars, March 1997.

PAGE 249
With Jim Carrey in the film *Man on the Moon*. Photographs by François Duhamel, 1999.

PAGES 250–51
"Sunset Marquis" lyrics, 2005.

PAGE 252
Courtney with Prince Andrew, ca. 1998.

PAGES 254–55
Photographs by Bruce Weber for the Versace men's campaign, 1997.

PAGE 256
"Bedroom Walls" lyrics, 2005.

PAGE 257
Photograph by Jean-Baptiste Mondino, May 2003. "How Dirty Girls Get Clean" lyrics.

PAGES 258–59
Courtney and Billy Corgan, and Courtney and Linda Perry—both photographs taken by Romy Suskin during recording sessions for Courtney's second solo album, *How Dirty Girls Get Clean*.

PAGE 261
Kurt Cobain and William S. Burroughs, in Lawrence, Kansas, 1993. Photograph by Courtney.

PAGE 262
Essay in diary, 2005.

PAGE 264
"Loser Dust" lyrics, 2005. Photograph by Jean-Baptiste Mondino, ca. 2002.

PAGE 265
"Stand Up Motherfucker" lyrics, 2006.

PAGES 266–67
"Man's Private World" poem, 2005.

PAGES 268–69
"The Depths of My Despair" lyrics, 2005. Photograph by Frank Micelotta.

PAGE 271
E-mail correspondence with Lindsay Lohan, 2006.

PAGES 272–83
Lyrics and diary entries, 2006.

PAGES 284–85
Photograph by Regan Cameron. Last page of self-made journal by "Aerie Rodriguez," aka Courtney Love, ca. 1974.

PERMISSIONS ACKNOWLEDGMENTS